CW00486438

DE HAVILLAND
COMET

1949–97 (all marks)

To the memory of
Alison Jane Martinez de las Rivas
(1951–2015)

© Brian Rivas 2016

All rights reserved. No part of this publication may be reproduced or stored in a retrieval system or transmitted, in any form or by any means, electronic, mechanical, photocopying, recording or otherwise, without prior permission in writing from Haynes Publishing.

First published in June 2016

A catalogue record for this book is available from the British Library.

ISBN 978 0 85733 832 7

Library of Congress control no. 2016930195

Published by Haynes Publishing,
Sparkford, Yeovil,
Somerset BA22 7JJ, UK.
Tel: 01963 440635
Int. tel: +44 1963 440635
Website: www.haynes.co.uk

Haynes North America Inc.,
861 Lawrence Drive, Newbury Park,
California 91320, USA.

Printed in the USA by Odcombe Press LP,
1299 Bridgestone Parkway,
La Vergne, TN 37086.

Copy editor: Michelle Tilling
Proof reader: Penny Housden
Indexer: Peter Nicholson
Page design: James Robertson

COVER IMAGE: de Havilland Comet 1.
(Mike Badrocke)

Acknowledgements

I started work on this book while my wife, Alison, was dying. It gave her comfort to know that I would have this project to focus on after her death, and she supported me in her characteristically courageous and selfless way until the end of her days. There are no words to express my love and gratitude.

As usual, my grateful thanks to Barry Guess and Trevor Friend of BAE Systems Heritage at Farnborough for allowing me to browse through and make selections from their 2,513 Comet images.

Prolific aviation writer and former de Havilland man Philip J. Birtles kindly invited me to peruse his impressive collection of Comet photographs, some of which have never previously been published. I owe him a debt of gratitude for allowing me to reproduce some of them.

My thanks to Peter Gill of www.flight-manuals-on-cd.com Ltd for the use of line drawings and schematics from *The de Havilland Comet Pilot's Notes*.

Whatever aircraft one is researching, it's a safe bet that the late Captain Eric 'Winkle' Brown had flown it, and the Comet 4 was one of them. As he did with much of my research, Eric gave his frank impressions of the pilot's view.

Andrew Clarke's recollections of his tenure with 216 Squadron were invaluable, as were the loan of his Comet advertisements and other documentation.

I would like to thank Professor Brian Clarkson for his enthusiastic help from his experience as a vibrations analyst in de Havilland's Structures Department.

My friend Jonathan Falconer, senior commissioning editor for aviation and military titles at Haynes Publishing, was always on hand with moral support and the ability from his decades of knowledge to point me in the right direction.

I owe a debt of gratitude for the usual unstinting help and publicity given by Roger de Mercado of The de Havilland Aeronautical Technical School Association, to the late senior de Havilland aerodynamicist John Wimpenny and his wife, Angela, for their friendship and support, and to the late David Newman, former chief aerodynamicist of de Havilland.

All of these kind people helped to make this project so fulfilling.

DE HAVILLAND COMET

1949–97 (all marks)

Owners' Workshop Manual

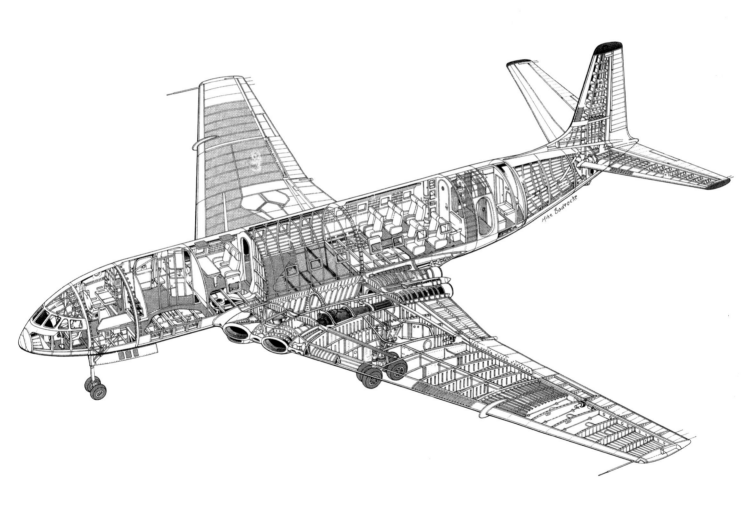

An insight into the design, construction and operation
of the world's first jet airliner

Brian Rivas

Contents

OPPOSITE A passenger's eye-view of the port wing and pinion fuel tank of a BOAC Comet 4C. *(PRM Aviation)*

Introduction

This is the story of an aircraft that blazed a trail for modern air travel, the beautiful de Havilland Comet. It is a story of triumph and tragedy, of a company that held faith in its darkest hour, and how the legacy of the Comet lived on into the 21st century.

OPPOSITE **Hours from its maiden flight, the prototype Comet (G-5-1) undergoes engine runs at Hatfield on 27 July 1949.** *(BAE Systems)*

When the first photographs of the de Havilland Comet appeared in newspapers in the summer of 1949, the world was taken by storm at the sight of this breathtakingly beautiful aircraft. A wave of pride swelled across Great Britain, for battered and bruised though we were after the long years of war, this surely showed that we led the world in aviation technology.

Our own Frank Whittle was famous for his pioneering work on the jet engine and de Havilland chief test pilot John Cunningham held the world altitude record. We were riding high – and now we were about to revolutionise air travel with the world's first jet airliner. But the Comet became the first to fly by only two weeks: had it not been for delays in completing a runway and carrying out repairs to an engine nacelle, the Avro Canada C102 Jetliner would have taken to the air first.

However, this aircraft was nothing like as revolutionary as the Comet, and apart from having four jet engines it looked very similar to typical piston engine airliners of the time. It could never have captured the public's imagination in the same way as the Comet, and it never even went into production.

During the war military requirements had to be the priority in England, but the war would not go on for ever and some thought had to be given to what kind of civil aircraft would be needed when hostilities ended. There was concern that Britain could be left behind more than she already was; even in 1939 the vast majority of the world's airline passengers were flying in Douglas DC-3 Dakotas.

An obvious interim measure was to convert bombers to carry passengers, which basically

BELOW The classic beauty of a BOAC Comet 1 in an English summer sky. *(British Airways)*

required little more than redesigning the inside of the fuselage, and among the results were the Avro York and Avro Lancastrian, which had their origins in the Lancaster. These were lumbering, noisy and uncomfortable beasts, and they were to become an embarrassment when America began operating the double-deck Boeing 377 Stratocruiser – itself developed from the wartime B-29 bomber – which had a pressurised cabin, could seat more than 100 passengers and had sleeping berths. Even its gracefully rounded nose, receding chin and high cockpit seemed to give it an air of smug superiority.

Anything but super

The best we could come up with was what was billed as 'a super plane from Avro'.

This was the Tudor, and it was anything but 'super', plagued as it was by aerodynamic and other problems; and it suffered a number of fatal accidents, including two aircraft lost in unexplained circumstances over the notorious Bermuda Triangle.

By the end of 1951 the passenger fleet of BOAC (British Overseas Airways Corporation, now British Airways) consisted of 22 Canadair Argonauts, 10 Boeing Stratocruisers, 10 Lockheed Constellations and 16 Handley Page Hermes IVs. Out of a total of 58 aircraft only 16 were British, so the Comet arrived just when our civil aviation needed a mighty shot in the arm. There is no question but that it set the scene for modern air travel, and even today it remains one of the most beautiful and iconic aircraft ever built.

There was no precedent for the Comet: by

BELOW
Photographers get a lens-ful of BOAC's Comet 2 (G-AMXD) as she comes in low over the airfield boundary.
(Copyright unknown)

flying twice as high and cruising almost twice as fast as conventional types, it was going where no airliner had gone before and would be entering uncharted territory. Flying at an altitude of up to 40,000ft meant that the hull had to be pressurised far higher than airliners that ventured barely beyond 20,000ft. The obvious dangers of this were well known to the de Havilland team, and in an article on design considerations chief designer Ronald E. Bishop said that the hull had to be built like a submarine – so strong that it could never rupture.

With this in mind, de Havilland thought they had everything covered; but time and tragedy were to prove them wrong, for there were stresses and hazards at play that were not understood at the time. Yet in spite of the failings for which it has inevitably been remembered, the Comet had a number of brilliant system innovations that remain standard on airliners to this day.

Exhaustive flight trials of the Comet prototypes went smoothly under the leadership of Cunningham, and elaborate rigs and procedures were set up for flight crew training. Everything was leading up to the historic day of 2 May 1952, when the world's first jet airliner service was inaugurated at London Airport as G-ALYP took off, bound for Johannesburg.

Speed records

From that moment onwards all the old piston engine types seemed to be from the age of gaslight. Air travel had entered a new and exciting era, and things would never be the same again. Passengers marvelled at the comparative silence, the extraordinary smoothness, the comfort and the unaccustomed feeling of not being tired at the end of a long flight. Impressive new speed records were set and everyone wanted to fly on the Comet – the rich, the famous and anyone else who could afford a ticket.

This was a serious wake-up call to the rest of the world, and orders began to pour in as Britain basked in a glow of aeronautical pride.

But the pride was short-lived, as accidents began to happen. Some were easily explained, but crucially there were two mysterious and shocking crashes in which Comets disintegrated at high altitude and fell into the sea with total loss of life. The whole fleet was grounded and an intense investigation was set up at Farnborough, which became a template for future accident investigations. Metal fatigue in relation to aircraft had received little attention

BELOW **Comet G-ALYP at Hatfield. This aircraft made the first scheduled jet airliner passenger flight on 2 May 1952.** *(Copyright unknown)*

ABOVE **A meeting of pioneers: Comet 4 G-APDA taxies past the Alcock and Brown memorial at London Airport in 1958.** *(British Airways)*

until then, but suddenly it was right in the spotlight. The information gleaned was of huge benefit to aircraft designers the world over.

But no one wanted to travel by Comet any longer, and the Comet 1 never operated as a passenger service again. The disasters allowed America to take the lead in jet airliners with their Boeing 707. It wasn't pretty like the Comet, but it could carry a lot more passengers and its engines were easy to maintain, being slung inelegantly but pragmatically and more safely under the wings.

Yet things were far from over for the Comet. Bowed but nowhere near beaten, it entered service again in the guise of the stretched and strengthened Comet 4, which had the distinction of inaugurating the first jet passenger service across the Atlantic with BOAC in 1958, beating the Boeing 707 to this record by just a few weeks; and it went on to give safe travel for many years with numerous airlines overseas and at home.

Meanwhile, military versions proliferated, most

notably the maritime Nimrod, which gave decades of service from 1969 until it was scrapped in 2011 in what was described in *The Economist* as 'one of the most extraordinary fiascos in the history of British defence procurement'.

The Comet story was marked by triumphs and tragedies – and finally in the case of the Nimrod by a complete debacle – but the original Comet was a pioneering and courageous design that opened the way forwards, and it remains a testament to the de Havilland team from the 1940s that the basic wing design remained in service for 60 years. They paid a terrible price for a design that was ahead of its time, and so did many innocent passengers, but the result was the safe and fast travel that we enjoy today. It was a leap that someone had to make.

Chapter One

The Comet story

──(●)──────

'Iconic' has become an over-used word, but in the context of the de Havilland Comet it is surely justified. The world's first jet airliner will be remembered for its grace and beauty, its speed and – inevitably – its tragic accidents. It was a pioneering design with a fatal flaw, but it is a tribute to the faith in this remarkable aircraft that it rose from the ashes as a bigger and better design to be loved and revered once again by passengers in the new era of jet travel.

OPPOSITE Ahead of its time, ahead of the world – the future arrived in 1949 with the prototype Comet. *(Getty Images)*

ABOVE **Geoffrey de Havilland prepares for his first attempt at flight in his home-built aircraft at Seven Barrows in Hampshire in November 1909. It ended in a crash, but his second flight was more successful – a few inches off the ground and a distance of 20 yards – but it was the start of great things.**
(Copyright unknown)

Genesis

In the early stages of the Second World War all aircraft design and production in England was of necessity focused on military requirements. Even de Havilland moved out of their comfort zone of beautiful airliners and delightful light aircraft to concentrate on a war machine, and this they did with spectacular success in the shape of the brilliant multi-role Mosquito. de Havilland had always been a classic example of thinking outside the box.

But after three years of hostilities the government felt it was high time to consider the kind of airliners that might be needed in peacetime. It didn't seem to have occurred to anyone that we might not win the war.

The first stirrings were in December 1942 when the Brabazon Committee met for initial discussions. Set up specifically to formulate proposals for civil aircraft, it was headed by aviation pioneer J.T.C. Moore-Brabazon (later Lord Brabazon of Tara), and included Captain Geoffrey de Havilland (founder of the de Havilland Aircraft Company). Britain could not afford to be left behind in the vitally important civil aviation market – America was way ahead with its wartime transport designs – and early in 1943 the committee presented its report to the government for five categories of civil aircraft which it was felt would cover all post-war needs.

As a stop-gap measure wartime military bombers were to be converted to airliners, but the word 'luxury' did not come into it: the incessant noise and vibration of, for example, four Rolls-Royce Merlin engines left passengers frazzled at the end of a long and slow journey. As for the Avro 688 Tudor, the less said the better. It was a hotch-potch that was beset

RIGHT To this – in just 40 years. A classic study of the first prototype Comet (G-5-1) on an early test flight on 5 August 1949.
(DH4233C/ BAE Systems)

with handling and other problems that resulted in service delays, and it could carry very few passengers – yet for some obscure reason the Ministry of Civil Aviation continued to subsidise this travesty, which sadly took the life of its designer, Roy Chadwick, in a take-off accident that was caused by incorrectly assembled aileron controls.

The Brabazon Committee continued to meet, and some of their proposals were later to evolve into successful airliners, such as the Vickers Viscount and Bristol Britannia, but it was Type IV that presented the most ambitious challenge: 'a jet-propelled mail-plane for the North Atlantic' cruising at 400mph. The committee's technical adviser from the Ministry of Aircraft Production, Dr Harold Roxbee-Cox, favoured turboprops, even though they had not yet been developed and would be very complex, but his calculations showed that for long range they would perform much better than piston engines at altitudes well above turbulent weather, and there was some doubt as to whether the thirsty and inefficient jet engines of the time would be capable of crossing the Atlantic.

But Captain de Havilland's forceful argument eventually won the day, for he had great confidence in the jet, especially in developments being made under Major Frank Halford at the

firm's own engine division. He did not feel there was anything to be gained by embarking on a conventional piston engine airliner, as it would inevitably be a few years behind American designs; the only answer was to leapfrog current technology. And the enormous prestige of being the first country with an operational jet airliner was not lost on the Air Ministry, while de Havilland knew that it would be hugely popular with air travellers.

ABOVE Captain Geoffrey de Havilland during the First World War. *(Copyright unknown)*

LEFT Flying for fun: Geoffrey de Havilland and his eldest son, Geoffrey Raoul, wind up their rubber-powered models. *(DH8356A/BAE Systems)*

BELOW The DH60 Moth, one of the most famous de Havilland designs from the golden inter-war years. *(Copyright unknown)*

RIGHT Geoffrey de Havilland pictured during the Second World War with a model of the company's legendary Mosquito. In the foreground is a large model of the Flamingo, while mounted high up is the elegant Albatross airliner. *(BAE Systems)*

RIGHT A classic shot of chief designer R.E. Bishop with the prototype Comet (G-5-1). *(Courtesy Dick Bishop)*

BELOW One of the most beautiful and shapely airliners ever built, the de Havilland DH91 Albatross. *(Copyright unknown)*

de Havilland were confident that the daunting requirement could be met, and in April 1944 the firm presented its proposals to the committee for a commercial jet airliner, which received their endorsement. However, there was no question at that stage of a pure jet being able to tackle the transatlantic route, which would require longer runways for the greater take-off distance; and the committee recommended an immediate start on the jet to be followed up with a twin-turboprop design for longer distances.

And so the die was cast: the prospect of a British jet airliner was now a reality.

Early birds that never flew ...

Even in 1941, before the Brabazon Committee first met, de Havilland had been considering a twin-Goblin jet engine version of their Flamingo airliner, but this was never proceeded with. After the company's first jet aircraft, the famous DH100 Vampire, took to the air in 1943, the idea evolved that a much larger version could be designed: an airliner powered by four Goblins grouped around the rear of the nacelle. It would carry 1,000lb of mail, but only six passengers. This idea was also dismissed – Bishop thought it was 'a stupid aeroplane'.

Later the same year a three-engine 20-passenger version was considered, and a scale model was wind tunnel tested at the Royal Aircraft Establishment (RAE), Farnborough. It was this proposal that was recommended by the Brabazon Committee, which in 1944 downgraded the Type IV proposal as no longer requiring transatlantic capability; instead it would operate on Empire routes. By this stage the project was known officially as the Brabazon IVB, and at de Havilland as the DH106 – but shortly afterwards came a complete change of direction.

As the advanced work in Germany into swept wings and tailless designs became known immediately after the war, Bishop and his team made a close study of the findings following his and chief aerodynamicist Richard Clarkson's visit to Germany for a first-hand look at some of the work achieved. They donned RAF uniforms and were careful to salute, bow and scrape in all the right places – but they

RIGHT The multi-role Mosquito, the wooden wonder. This was an example of de Havilland's pragmatic approach to aircraft concept and design. It was treated with derision by the top brass – until they saw it flying. The rest is history.
(Copyright unknown)

were shocked at what they found, and decided excitedly that a swept-wing tailless jet could form the basis of an airliner powered by four de Havilland Ghost engines, the Ghost being a more powerful development of the Goblin.

The outline for this hugely ambitious proposal was for an aircraft with an all-up weight of 75,000lb that would carry 24 passengers in eight rows of three seats, wings swept to 40°, no horizontal tail surfaces and the engines mounted in pairs either side of the fuselage beneath the wing and near the trailing edge. At one point a canard design had been considered, but at that time it presented insurmountable aerodynamic problems, as well as looking rather odd.

... and one that did

The concept of a jet-powered tailless airliner was without precedent – it would look futuristic even today – and the Ministry of Aviation accepted that extensive evaluation and testing would be needed to prove the format, so in January 1945 Air Staff Requirement OR.207 Specification E.18/45 was issued for the design

LEFT After the Mosquito came the Vampire jet fighter, and the first study for the Comet was based on a similar twin-boom format.
(Copyright unknown)

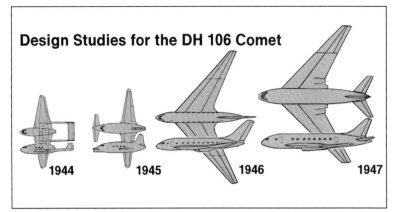

Design Studies for the DH 106 Comet

1944   1945   1946   1947

LEFT Early design studies for the DH106 Comet. The first (left) was based on the Vampire, but was discarded. The second was more radical, and certainly rather odd-looking, but the canard format presented difficult aerodynamic problems at the time. Next came the swept-wing tailless concept, which was tested on the one-third scale DH108, but was abandoned even before the 108 flew. Then came a similar design, but with a tailplane – but even this would not have been economical, and the outcome was an aircraft of much more conventional appearance.

and construction of two approximately third-scale prototypes – one for low-speed testing, the other for speeds of up to 650mph and Mach 0.9 (90% of the speed of sound).

The result was the swept-wing tailless DH108, which bore more than a passing resemblance to the German wartime rocket-powered Messerschmitt Me163 Komet. One version was to investigate low-speed handling, while the other would probe high Mach numbers. Ironically, by the time the first prototype (TG/283) flew on 15 May 1946 at the hands of Geoffrey de Havilland Jr, the design team had abandoned the tailless concept, as calculations had shown that using ailerons as elevators, with their small lever arm from the

ABOVE A classic study of Geoffrey de Havilland Jr, who would lose his life in a DH108 (TG306) at the age of 36. *(DH2411E/ BAE Systems)*

RIGHT General arrangement drawing of the Comet 1. It looked futuristic for its time, but was less extreme than some of the earlier design studies. *(www.flight-manuals-on-cd.com)*

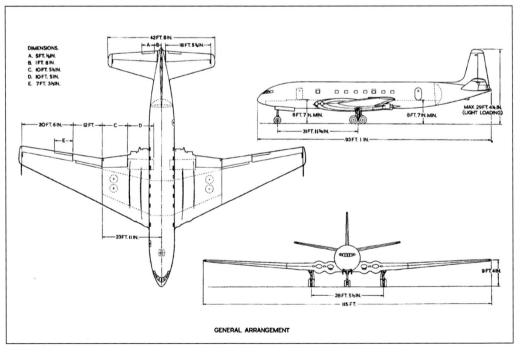

GENERAL ARRANGEMENT

centre of gravity, would limit the effectiveness of flaps on the inner wing, so that for a given runway length the take-off and landing weight would have to be a lot lower than with a tailplane and conventional elevators.

By the end of May the provisional plan was for a four-jet aircraft with horizontal tail surfaces and wings swept to 40°, an all-up weight of 93,000lb and a maximum Atlantic payload of 5,000lb, but in July further calculations showed that substituting conventional wings would allow the payload almost to be doubled to 9,200lb. This was because of the considerably lower weight and greater lift efficiency of straight wings.

As far as a test-bed for the Comet platform was concerned, the 108 was largely redundant before it started, and the project was switched to pure research into swept wings. But a lot was learned over nearly 500 flights, some of which was useful for the Comet – especially low-speed handling where swept wings run into problems, and the characteristics of powered flying controls – but at a terrible cost: young Geoffrey was killed on the evening of 27 September 1946 when the second prototype (TG306) disintegrated in a high-speed dive while he was working up for an attempt on the world airspeed record.

Up to that point it had been a day of celebration for the company. Following a

ABOVE **The first of the three DH108 tailless jets (TG283) designed to investigate the low- and high-speed characteristics of swept wings.** *(DH2292A/BAE Systems)*

BELOW **Sprouting wing fences and an extra droop over the air intake, the low-speed DH108 (TG283) in one of its many configurations to explore stalling characteristics of the swept wing.** *(DH3092B/BAE Systems)*

ABOVE Senior aerodynamicist John Wimpenny (left) and John Cunningham discuss the results of a DH108 test flight. Cunningham's most frightening moments in the air were in this aircraft. (BAE Systems)

BELOW The de Havilland Ghost engine as used in the Comet 1. (DH3959E/ BAE Systems)

conversation with BOAC, Geoffrey's father was told that detail design on the DH106 could go ahead. It was what de Havilland had been waiting for – now nothing would stand in their way of building the world's first jet airliner for commercial passenger service.

After young Geoffrey's death, Cunningham took over as chief test pilot and TG306 was replaced by a second high-speed prototype (VW120), in which de Havilland test pilot John Derry set a new 100km closed circuit speed record and later became the first British pilot to crack the so-called sound barrier on 6 September 1948 in a wildly out-of-control dive.

In 1950 this aircraft was also lost at high speed, taking the life of RAE Farnborough test pilot Stuart Muller-Rowland, and weeks later

TG283 spun and crashed at Hartley Wintney in Hampshire, killing another young RAE pilot, Eric 'Jumbo' Genders.

At both ends of the speed envelope it was a twitchy and capricious aircraft to handle – hardly ideal for an airliner – and by the time Geoffrey lost his life detailed design work on the Comet was under way in secrecy at de Havilland's headquarters at Hatfield, Hertfordshire.

By the end of 1946 the design of the airliner had been firmed up, although it was not until December the following year that it was officially known as the Comet. It looked streamlined and graceful, with a projected all-up weight of 100,000lb; but with wings swept to only a mild 20° at quarter chord and a conventional tailplane it had a far less radical appearance than the original tailless concept. One challenge facing wing designer Bill Tamblin was ensuring wing strength and integrity at the roots, where there were four tunnels to house the Ghost engines.

Design considerations

The Comet was to operate in hostile atmospheric environments where no airliner had gone before. The problems were huge: for example, pressurising a large cabin at 40,000ft with constantly changing air at far higher internal levels of stress than had ever been achieved, together with careful control over temperature and humidity; flying routinely in extremely low temperatures with unknown effects on materials; navigation and traffic control at high speed; good handling characteristics at low speed; and landing without the braking effect of propellers.

Central to the Comet was the powerplant. At the time there were two types of jet engine – centrifugal, such as the de Havilland Goblin and more powerful Ghost, and axial flow, the best-known early example being the Rolls-Royce Avon which was under development. Both had advantages and disadvantages, but as far as the Comet was concerned de Havilland's own engines were the obvious initial choice – not simply because they were a proven design, but also because no one had at that point succeeded in de-icing an axial engine, and neither had any trials been done on tapping the blower for pressure-cabin air or bleeding off air for de-icing the flying surfaces. However,

LEFT Two burning, two not turning: Avro Lancastrian VM703 testing Ghost engines for the Comet project. *(DH2901I/BAE Systems)*

even at the earliest design stages an axial flow engine had been envisaged at some point in the airliner's development, and was discussed with de Havilland by BOAC as early as 1946.

The decision was to use the Ghost on the Comet 1 and Avons on later marks. Because of the moderate wing-loading – less than some piston engine airliners – 'stretched' versions had already been contemplated. To wait for the Avon would have resulted in a considerable delay before the aircraft entered service, as the engine had some way to go before it was certificated for civil operation. And so the Comet was designed around four Ghost engines which would be housed elegantly in the wing roots – although at that point even the Ghost had not received civil approval.

The original plan was to have a fuselage about the size of a Douglas DC-3 Dakota with a diameter of 8ft 6in and seating for 24 passengers, but the more the design team studied the various issues the more confident they felt about going for a full-size hull to accommodate about 40 – something for which BOAC had lobbied.

The intention from the outset was that, like the Mosquito, the Comet would go straight into production off the drawing board in parallel with the first two prototypes, which would be used for the main test programme. This was important, for it would save at least two years – but it also prevented the firm from embarking on any ideas that were too advanced: they had to get it right first time to avoid any costly and time-consuming redesign. As Bishop put it:

'It meant that we had to reach sufficiently far ahead in design to take good advantage of the new form of power unit, but not so far as to involve ourselves in highly experimental features. In every way the design must represent a logical step forward.'

BOAC were eager to have this revolutionary aircraft in their fleet and placed an advance order for eight Comets, a deal negotiated by de Havilland business and sales manager Francis E.N. St Barbe. Six more were ordered by British South African Airways (BSAA), which later merged with BOAC. But de Havilland had to give contractual guarantees under penalty relating to performance and delivery date, and agree the price in advance. Based as it was on 1946 prices, this was a commercial risk for

BELOW The rudimentary but accurate replica of the Comet nose spliced on to a Horsa glider, which conveniently was the same diameter. *(DH3851B/ BAE Systems)*

ABOVE John Cunningham tested a Comet nose replica grafted on to a Horsa glider to be certain that visibility was satisfactory under various weather conditions. *(DH2605E/BAE Systems)*

ABOVE Makeshift but effective: de Havilland's method of trialling the Comet's steerable nose wheel *(DH3191E/BAE Systems)*

BELOW The Horsa with the Comet nose was towed aloft by this Handley Page Halifax (PP389). Much of this work was done during the harsh winter of 1946–47. *(DH2605C/BAE Systems)*

de Havilland, one that would not amount to a break-even figure; but they felt it was justifiable.

And they owed BOAC a debt of gratitude, for the Corporation had been firmly behind the jet airliner concept from the earliest Brabazon Committee meetings and had made its support known to the various ministries. Had it not been for the enthusiastic backing by the technical team and chairman Lord Knollys, the project could well have been deemed too revolutionary for a cautious English committee and might never have got off the ground.

Weight and strength

The first hurdle in the drawing office was every designer's nightmare: weight. As the payload of the Comet would be little more than 10% of the all-up weight at take-off, every effort had to be made to keep the weight of the airframe, systems and ancillaries to an absolute minimum without sacrificing strength and integrity. This was a difficult balancing act. Every component, however small, was examined to see how weight could be saved, for it would have been all too easy to get into a spiral of more weight needing more power, more power resulting in more weight and so on, until the whole proposition became impractical.

During the war de Havilland had been using a metal-to-metal bonding process called Redux, a contraction of 'Research at Duxford', where the inventors, Aero Research Ltd, were based. It was a two-part process using pheno-formaldehyde and a white powder of polyvinyl-formal plastic known as 'Formvar'. It had been used successfully on the de Havilland

Hornet during the war as well as on the Dove light transport in 1945, so was the obvious choice on the Comet, where it would not only give great strength but a smooth surface to minimise drag and considerable weight-saving by dispensing with many thousands of rivets.

It could be used in double-curvature applications, so was equally suitable for fuselage as well as wing construction. Its great bonding power meant that thinner-gauge skinning could be used with no loss of strength, and parts of the Comet fuselage were covered in remarkably thin aluminium sheet, about the thickness of a postcard.

To keep weight and drag to a minimum, Bishop went for the smallest fuselage diameter that would accommodate two passengers in reasonable comfort either side of the central aisle. This worked out at 10ft. One of the most striking features of the fuselage was the cockpit windscreen, which was gracefully formed into the flowing lines of the nose section. There was some doubt as to whether this would give adequate visibility from the flight deck, so tests were carried out on a wartime troop-carrying Airspeed Horsa glider which was fitted with a mock-up of the Comet cockpit. It so happened that the diameter of the glider's fuselage was the same as the rear frame of the Comet's nose, so the adaptation was simple. Tests were also done in bad weather to check the effect of rain while landing at low speeds. All was satisfactory.

But the major challenge with the fuselage, and one that Bishop said 'caused us considerable worry', was carrying fare-paying passengers at a height of 40,000ft in comfort and safety. Because it had never been done before, de Havilland embarked on the most exhaustive series of testing in the history of aviation – not just on the fuselage, but on every part of the aircraft.

With a temperature at this height that can dip to below –50°C, cabin heating and insulation were vitally important. This is where the jet engine had a great advantage in that hot air under pressure could be tapped from the main engine compressor, thus doing away with the bulky and heavy blowers and combustion heaters used on piston engine types. So temperature control on the Comet was actually accomplished by cooling rather than heating the incoming air, even at those altitudes.

Biggest challenge

But by far the biggest challenge was pressurising the hull. At such altitudes it would have to be approximately double that used on conventional airliners operating at about 20,000ft. The stresses involved would be massive.

As Bishop put it in an article in a special edition of *The Aeroplane* published on 2 May 1952 to mark the day of the world's first jet passenger service: 'The consequences of a pressure cabin failure would be so serious that the fuselage must be designed rather like a submarine, so that it would never fail.'

With this in mind, elaborate test-rigs were constructed at Hatfield, but using air pressure was both unsatisfactory and unsafe. Not only was there the danger of flying debris if the hull ruptured, but it would be difficult to locate the exact point of failure, and so a special water tank was built in which large fuselage sections were immersed and then pressurised with water. One of these was 26ft long, the other 24ft, but at no point was a complete hull tested; and this was to have a significance that was not foreseen.

It was the first time such a test tank had been built in Britain, and it demonstrated the lengths to which the company went to ensure they had an aeroplane that exceeded all statutory requirements – but they could only work with the knowledge that was then available.

Testing to destruction

'We adopted a policy of testing every part of the pressure cabin to destruction,' wrote Bishop, 'and never relying entirely upon calculations. We employed factors on the pressure part of

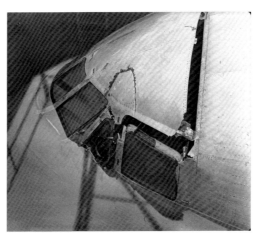

LEFT **Testing to destruction: de Havilland were well aware of the hazards of routinely flying a pressurised hull at 40,000ft and carried out exhaustive tests to ensure the aircraft's safety. But dynamics were at play that they did not know about.** (DH3851B/BAE Systems)

LEFT Exhaustive pressure tests were carried out on fuselage sections. This is one that failed in April 1948 after many overloads in the water tank. These tests were very thorough, but no one realised that they did not replicate real-world conditions. *(DH3333C/BAE Systems)*

CENTRE A foretaste of things to come. Skin failure around a window of a Comet fuselage section that was tested to destruction by de Havilland in June 1948. *(DH3418B/BAE Systems)*

the fuselage considerably higher than those demanded by the Airworthiness Requirement.'

For passenger comfort and well-being at 40,000ft it was necessary to simulate conditions equivalent to an altitude of 8,000ft, and this required a cabin pressure of 8¼lb/sq in – more than twice that of conventional airliners. No chances could be taken, so a safety factor of 2½ was built in, which equated to 20¼lb/sq in. Test specimens were subjected to 16½lb/sq in, and all fuselage sections to 11lb/sq in.

Pressurisation cycles were carried out thousands of times, thought to be the equivalent of around 40,000 hours of typical flying, and the whole structural test programme was conducted in the belief that repeated large overloads in static testing would cover any stresses in service.

The windows were seen as a potential weak spot and were treated as a special case. Many tests were carried out, including pressurising them every working day for three years – even to the extent of cleaning and polishing them twice a week with scratch-remover in case this could have any effect on the glazing's ability to withstand stress. One window was subjected to a load of 100lb/sq in without failure.

The Air Registration Board (ARB), responsible for issuing certificates of airworthiness to civil aircraft, was quoted as saying that explosive decompression at 40,000ft 'shouldn't happen

LEFT Another view of the rupture during de Havilland's pressure tests. Apart from the damage to the side of the fuselage, the stringers have completely separated from the bulkhead. *(DH3303E/BAE Systems)*

any oftener [*sic*] than a wing falling off'. How wrong this was to be.

Another safety factor on which Bishop insisted was that all cabin access doors and hatches would open inwards, so that when closed they would form an increasingly airtight plug as pressure built up. Being able to tap the engines to supply air to the hull was a further safety bonus. Not only did it save weight but it meant that the system was duplicated three times, as any one engine could maintain the necessary pressure.

As with the fuselage, the wing came in for some equally punishing tests. With a constant thickness to chord ratio of 11%, it was relatively thin, and every effort was made to keep drag as low as possible. The Comet did not have aerials sprouting from the airframe; instead they were buried within the fuselage.

The first production wing was fixed to a section of fuselage, and the tip was deflected by 3ft many thousands of times by hydraulic rams. It withstood this with no problems.

Landing loads

The main undercarriage was mounted on the same rig and subjected to the worst possible landing loads thousands of times – a test not just for the undercarriage assembly but the surrounding wing structure. Drag and side loads were also applied as well as drop and retraction tests, while 16,000 retractions were made with the bearings packed with grease and sand.

The main wheels on the two prototypes were not elegant – just a single large one under each wing – but for production Comets this was changed to four smaller wheels in a bogie configuration. These not only lessened the load on runways but were much safer in the event of a tyre blow-out, and they were trialled on one of the prototype aircraft.

Most British aircraft at this time were 'tail-sitters', so there was little experience with a steerable nose wheel. de Havilland improvised a very simple but effective test by taking a 3-ton commercial lorry chassis and mounting a Comet nose wheel and ballast at the front with a pair of Mosquito main wheels as outriggers. It was a weird-looking contraption as it trundled along the Hatfield runway like some bizarre tricycle,

often with a trilby-hatted Sir Geoffrey (he was knighted after the war) on board, but it covered 120 miles at up to nearly 50mph and proved that the nose wheel operation was sound.

Materials and controls

How would conventional materials used in aircraft construction stand up to several hours of flying in temperatures that would be around –50°C and possibly lower? To find out, de Havilland built a special decompression chamber capable of taking a full-diameter Comet fuselage section and simulating conditions up to 70,000ft, where temperatures are down to –70°C. They soon found that materials used for bag tanks, flexible hoses and other common ancillaries were hopeless, as they became brittle, so a huge amount of development work was done before materials were found that could maintain reasonable flexibility for several hours at extreme altitudes.

Bearing in mind the airliner's speed and size, the team had decided from the outset to use powered flying controls on the Comet, and some experience of these was gained on the DH108. Conventional aerodynamically balanced controls could have been used, but these would have been heavier to operate and would have taken a great deal of flying time to get right, whereas powered controls could be set up accurately on the firm's ground test-rig known as 'iron bird'. This was done in the factory, and a full-size Comet control system was built and operated for more than three years.

ABOVE A meeting of three aviation greats: de Havilland chief test pilot John Cunningham, jet engine pioneer Frank Whittle and Major Frank Halford, chairman and director of the de Havilland Engine Company, pictured under the rear fuselage of the prototype Comet. *(Getty Images)*

ABOVE **Two days before her first flight, prototype G-5-1 undergoes some checks and adjustments. Also in the picture is a de Havilland Mosquito.** *(BAE Systems)*

BELOW **John Walker (left), engine installation designer, and Bill Tamblin, wing designer, chatting beneath a Comet's air intakes.** *(DH4246C/BAE Systems)*

Another advantage of power controls was that larger control surfaces with greater angular travel could be used. However, one problem that John Derry found in his long test programme on the high-speed 108 was that some form of artificial feel was desirable for the pilot, and this involved a lot of trial and error.

The primary power control system on the Comet operated only the ailerons, elevators and rudder, while a secondary system actuated the undercarriage and flaps. All hydraulic rams and valves were duplicated and three separate hydraulic power supply systems for the flying controls were installed.

Before passing the Comet's system of irreversible power controls, the ARB had to be fully satisfied that a hydraulic piston could not jam in its cylinder, as such an event could cause control failure.

Fire precautions and fuel

With the engines buried in the wing adjacent to the hull, fire was a potential hazard, and stringent precautions were taken. The hot parts of the engines were isolated from the main structure by steel fireproof bulkheads, while the tailpipes were shrouded in steel tubes with cooling air passing down the annulus.

Detection systems were installed so that the crew would know instantly if fire had broken out and the pilot could shut off the fuel supply to the relevant engine. Bishop felt that one of the biggest steps to improve safety was the use of paraffin instead of petrol in jet engines, as this had a much lower fire risk.

Unless a fast and reliable means of pressure refuelling was developed, much of the Comet's speed advantage in the air would be lost on the ground. A system was devised, and used in the first prototype, that allowed the full capacity of 7,000gal to be replenished in 20min.

Engines

The Comet was to be fitted with de Havilland Ghost 50 engines, each producing 5,000lb static thrust, but extensive flight trials were necessary to explore optimum intake shapes, ram effect, fuel systems, engine re-lighting at altitude and jet-pipe temperatures.

An Avro Lancastrian (VM703), a civil version of the Lancaster bomber, was chosen for this, and its two outer Merlin piston engines were replaced with Ghosts, at that stage developing 4,450lb static thrust, while the two inner Merlins remained to assist with take-off and any emergency. It first flew in this form on 24 July 1947, and trials were carried out by Cunningham and de Havilland Engine Company chief test pilot Chris Beaumont. Hundreds of hours were flown with this aircraft, which was later joined by two others, and by the time the Ghost was ready to be installed in the Comet all teething troubles had been eliminated.

The only thing the Lancastrian couldn't do was check performance at the Comet's normal operating altitude, as its ceiling height was only 25,000ft. However, the engine's ability at great height was demonstrated on 23 March the following year when Cunningham took a Ghost-powered Vampire to 59,492ft, setting a new world altitude record for fixed wing aircraft.

The Lancastrian was used again in the civil certification procedures for the Ghost, the engine finally receiving approval from the ARB in July 1948.

Rockets

Serious consideration was given to rocket assisted take-off (RATO) for the Comet, as it was felt that its jet engines, with less immediate 'bite' on the air than propellers, might need some help in getting the aircraft airborne from hot, high runways overseas. de Havilland had already developed the Sprite hydrogen peroxide rocket motor, and tests were carried out with one on each wing mounted between the Ghosts of the prototype Comet, the first flight in this configuration being at

BELOW If you were a passenger and looked out of the window to see this happening on take-off, would you be alarmed? Probably you would. In the end, assistance from a pair of de Havilland Sprite rocket motors was not needed, but testing was spectacular, as this shot of Cunningham getting airborne on 10 May 1951 in the first Comet prototype shows. *(DH5501/BAE Systems)*

LEFT Sir Geoffrey de Havilland (left) with chief designer R.E. Bishop and Prince Philip in front of a Comet 1 at Hatfield. Photos of Bishop are rare, photos of him smiling are even more rare – and this is not one of them. *(DH6164I/BAE Systems)*

Hatfield on 7 May 1951. With its 5,000lb thrust, two Sprites represented two extra Ghosts, and with a burn duration of 12sec would be more than enough to get the Comet quickly off the ground in marginal atmospheric conditions.

A total of 32 take-offs were carried out successfully, and the sight of a Comet soaring skywards trailing two thunderous clouds of steam was spectacular. Perhaps more in hope than expectation, it was thought that passengers might not be too alarmed by this, but in the end the idea was abandoned as it was found that the Comet could cope without any extra help.

Another avenue considered was in-flight refuelling, and after getting some experience with a Meteor IV linking up with a Lancaster from Flight Refuelling Ltd, Cunningham flew prototype G-ALVG with a refuelling probe fitted; but after some experiments it was not considered practical for airliners.

One major advantage of the jet engine for passengers was the smoothness and lack of vibration compared to piston engines, but even so there would be considerable noise for anyone sitting next to the jet-pipes. After some experiments with a Vickers Viking powered by two Rolls-Royce Nene jets, two rows of seats in the Comet were moved from the back of the cabin to the front. In absolute terms the noise of a jet engine was not much less than a piston engine, but it was not so unpleasant – and certainly less fatiguing.

And so the design was finalised. With a length of 93ft 1in and a wingspan of 115ft, the Comet 1 would have an all-up weight of 105,000lb. The next step was to build a full-size wooden mock-up so that all internal fittings and fixtures could be determined.

The mainliner of the future

A new era in speed and comfort combined with economical operation and unprecedented mechanical simplicity

DE HAVILLAND COMET

LEFT The start of a new era in air travel: an early de Havilland advertisement for the Comet. *(Courtesy Andrew Clarke)*

COMET CHRONOLOGY

1943	Feb	First Brabazon Committee recommends development of jet-powered mail aircraft.
	June	Second Brabazon Committee recommends simple and easily developed Type IV of about 30,000lb all-up weight.
1944	Nov	Interim report of Brabazon Committee gives outline performance of de Havilland Type IV project.
1945	Sept	BOAC recommends development order for DH106.
	Dec	BOAC agrees to buy up to ten DH106.
1946	Aug	DH106 configuration agreed.
1947	Jan	Order for 16 DH106 placed – 2 prototypes and 14 aircraft for BOAC and BSAA. Full production initiated.
1948	June	BOAC circulates first project branch route analysis.
	July	Ghost engine receives Air Registration Board civil approval at 4,450lb thrust with 250hr inter-overhaul period. BOAC project engineer attached to de Havilland.
	Nov	Bogie-type undercarriage recommended by de Havilland.
1949	Mar	First details of Comet released.
	Apr	First Comet wheeled out for engine runs.
	27 July	Prototype Comet (G-ALVG) makes first flight (31min).
	22 Oct	First night-flying trials by Comet.
	25 Oct	First overseas flight of Comet to Castel Benito, Tripoli.
	14 Nov	First long-distance flight by Comet of 5hr 33min.
	Dec	Canadian Pacific Airlines' order for two Comets announced.
1950	12 Feb	First Comet flight using hull pressurisation.
	16 Mar	Point-to-point records broken on London–Rome–London flight – outward 447mph, homeward 453.5mph.
	24 Apr	Comet leaves for tropical trials. London–Cairo record made at 426.5mph.
	11 May	Comet returns from tropical trials. Cairo–London record made at 386mph.
	15 Jun	First prototype Comet completes 324hr of flying.
	27 July	Second prototype Comet (G-ALZK) makes first flight.
	Sept	BOAC Comet unit formed.
	1 Dec	Avon-engined Comet 2 announced.
1951	9 Jan	First production Comet (G-ALYP) makes first flight.
	2 Apr	Second prototype flown to BOAC for development flying by Comet Unit.
	May	Chargeurs Reunis SA order two Comet 1s from services from Paris to Africa and Indo-China.
	24 May	Comet G-ALZK leaves for first BOAC development flight to Cairo.
	17–18 July	First BOAC flight to Johannesburg.
	28 July	First flight of second production Comet (G-ALYR)
	8 Sept	First flight of third production Comet (G-ALYS)
	23 Sept	First BOAC ATC trials completed with night flights in normal airline conditions from London Airport.
	10 Oct	Twelfth and last BOAC development flight to Singapore and Djakarta.
	18 Oct	Return of Comet from final development flight after completing 470hr with BOAC.
	30 Oct	Chargeurs Reunis SA announce increased Comet 1 order to three, with option on Comet 2.
	Nov	Royal Canadian Air Force order for two Comet 1s announced.
	21 Nov	Air France order for three Comet 1s announced.
	31 Dec	British Commonwealth Pacific Airlines order for six Comet 2s announced. Fourth production Comet (G-ALYU) makes first flight. BOAC takes delivery of its first Comet (G-ALYS).
1952	22 Jan	Normal category Certificate of Airworthiness for the Comet handed over.
	16 Feb	First flight of prototype Avon-engined Comet 2 (G-ALYT). Airborne for 1hr 53min from Hatfield.
	3 Mar	Plans announced for production of Comet by Short Brothers and Harland.
	6 Mar	BOAC takes delivery of its second Comet (G-ALYU).
	23 Mar	BOAC takes delivery of its third Comet (G-ALYP).
	9 Apr	First flight of fifth production Comet (G-ALYV)
	23 Apr	BOAC takes delivery of its fourth Comet (G-ALYV)
	2 May	World's first passenger service in a jet airliner inaugurated as G-ALYP departs London Airport for Johannesburg.

Chapter Two

Building the Comet

When a delegation from Boeing visited Hatfield during Comet production, they thought the assembly line was more like a small town auto-repair shop compared to their massive B47 Stratojet bomber production facility in Seattle. It must have seemed that way to them – and yet the methods devised for building the Comet were outstanding examples of innovative engineering where minimum costs and maximum quality went hand in hand.

OPPOSITE One of G-ALYR's Ghost engines hooked up to its tailpipe. Also in the picture are the four wheels for the landing gear on the starboard wing. The strut can be seen under the wheel well waiting to be installed. *(DH6251/BAE Systems)*

RIGHT The de Havilland photographer seizes the chance to get a spot of glamour into the proceedings against the backdrop of G-ALYR. The woman was among a group of visitors who were shown around the factory on 15 September 1950 to see Comets being built. *(DH4994G/ BAE Systems)*

Some of the building and production techniques used on the wartime Mosquito had applications for the Comet project, and of particular importance was the close cooperation between the various departments, which was something that came naturally, as the company had always had a strong family feel in which everyone's views and inputs were considered.

Like the Mosquito, the two prototypes were to be built at the same time as the first production batch, so tooling had to be set up well in advance to get the prototypes completed as soon as possible.

Because a price had been agreed on the BOAC order, production on the initial batch of aircraft had to be done at a reasonable cost. This involved devising essential tooling and producing it within the deadlines at an expense that was justified by the contract price, but also to the very high standard that the Comet demanded. A major undertaking was the design and manufacture of the Reduxing tools for the extensive bonding processes used throughout the aircraft.

The objective was that there would be only a small gap between the prototype flying and the first machines coming off the production line, but in parallel with production would be the development of new processes and techniques not then fully established.

All this required a close and constant liaison between the drawing office, experimental section, test laboratory and production departments. As it turned out, it was not possible to achieve the aim of flying the first production aircraft six months after the prototype. This actually took a year, but de Havilland's production director, Harry Povey, did not regard this as a complete failure.

As he pointed out in a lecture to the Royal Aeronautical Society: 'To see the achievement against the planned programme, the fact had to be taken into account that the flying control system on the first production aircraft underwent extensive changes in design which, together with many other alterations, accounted for a delay of a few months.'

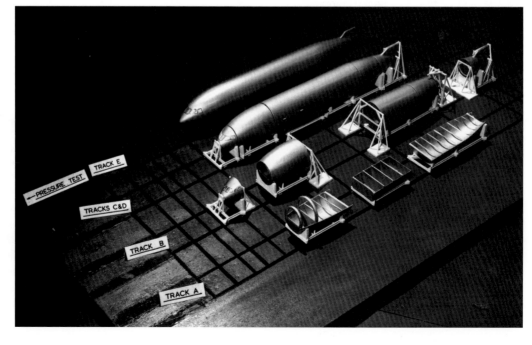

RIGHT A diorama showing fuselage components and order of assembly on the workshop floor tracks. *(DH5340E/ BAE Systems)*

RIGHT Jigs used for assembling large fuselage components, in this case for G-ALYZ . The window cut-outs can be seen on the rear skinned sections. *(DH5303C/BAE Systems)*

CENTRE Fuselage skin sections for BOAC Comets being set up on a jig in December 1949. The techniques at de Havilland must have seemed a bit of a joke to the American visitors from Boeing, where production of the B47 Stratojet six-jet bomber was under way on a big scale. However, America wasn't laughing when the Comet went into service. *(DH4451D/BAE Systems)*

Building techniques

The key to speedy and efficient production was the preparation of procedures and tools that would normally have been left to a later date. A very early decision, one that carried some risk for the design department, was tooling up the wing spar booms for milling well in advance.

Drop-hammer techniques and heavy tools were developed for the door jamb and door frames, window frames were also tooled on the drop-hammer and the hull pressure dome was produced from drop-hammer pressings. Three-stage drop-hammer tools were needed for the more complex nose section of the fuselage, and for the first time the company developed glass-cloth mouldings for the Comet, which involved some experimentation by the production department. This was invaluable for the production of small fibreglass components such as ducting and other piping, as very complex shapes could be manufactured easily with the added advantage of light weight and good resistance to moisture.

The method of making the main fuselage

RIGHT Early construction work on Comet fuselages in November 1950. Airframes being worked on are G-ALYW, YX, YY and YZ. The latter two were involved in accidents while in service: YZ failed to get airborne at Rome after the nose was raised too high, and YY was lost with all on board in a decompression disintegration in 1954. *(DH5154/BAE Systems)*

ABOVE The second Comet prototype (G-ALZK) in the autumn of 1949 with the stub-wing assembly attached to the fuselage. In the foreground the outer wing sections are being prepared before fitting to the stub assembly. On the left is the rear of the fuselage of G-ALYP. *(Copyright unknown)*

ABOVE Comets in various stages of construction at Hatfield in February 1950. The fuselages here are of G-ALYP, YR, YS, YT and ZK. *(DH4587L/BAE Systems)*

LEFT Another view of G-ALYP under construction in December 1950. Visible on the shop floor are the tracks which were used to transport major components to their assembly stations. *(Copyright unknown)*

rings was thought to be unique, and it was certainly the first time it had been used in Britain. Straight sections were produced in a set of standard rolls, and the sections were then formed by stretching and bending the rings of various radii on a Hufford stretch-forming machine. Costs were kept down by producing one basic tool which, by adding segments of different radius, adjusted the tool for all ring diameters. The rings were bent round the tool while under tension so that the webs of the 10ft 3in diameter rings were perfectly flat.

Plaster models were used for the development of drop-hammer, stretcher-press and Hufford tools on all major components. Plates were printed on sheet metal then cut out and assembled into three-dimensional structures, which were filled with plaster to provide accurate solid models from which most of the tooling was made.

LEFT Basic fitting out of the cabin on G-ALYP during September 1950. Care was taken by the designers to ensure that passengers did not feel as though they were sitting in a circular tube. *(DH5021A/BAE Systems)*

ABOVE Inside the rear fuselage section of
G-ALYS. *(DH4451I/BAE Systems)*

ABOVE RIGHT The pressure dome of G-ALYU.
This aircraft would later be used in the water tank
at Farnborough during the accident investigation.
(DH4584B/BAE Systems)

Wing-building and drilling jigs were
constructed, including a unit for the vitally
important mating of the wing centre section to
the fuselage. This involved the accurate drilling
of 252 tightly toleranced holes with special
radial drills. All jigs were produced as simply as
possible and designed to allow easy assembly
by the fitters.

The Redux process

Redux metal-to-metal bonding was used
on the Comet on a scale never before
attempted. The advantages of adhesives in
aerodynamic and construction terms were
huge, for no matter how well countersunk
riveting was carried out there would inevitably
be surface irregularities. In an aircraft as clean
as the Comet this could not be tolerated, and
the decision was taken to bond the skin panels
to the stringers on the fuselage, wings and tail
assembly. Only a minimum amount of riveting
would be used throughout the airframe.

With complete contact area between stringer
and skin there was a uniform distribution of
load, as opposed to the thousands of stress
concentrations that would be present from
rivets or spot welding; and without the need
for countersunk holes a much thinner gauge of
skin could be used with safety. The result was a

ABOVE A fine shot of G-ALYR on the shop floor. In the foreground is one of
its Ghost engines. *(Copyright unknown)*

BELOW The fuselage of the first prototype pictured on 7 May 1949.
(DH3385A/BAE Systems)

ABOVE Fuselages of G-ALYR, YS and YT at similar stages of build at Hatfield. (DH4128A/ BAE Systems)

BELOW The bare flight deck of G-ALYS, with the captain's control yoke in place. (DH4451K/BAE Systems)

BELOW RIGHT Stringers, formers, windows, skinning and part of the floor fitted to G-ALYS. (DH4451S/BAE Systems)

huge saving in weight. Less weight meant more payload; more payload meant more profit. Every little saving counted.

Another advantage was the superior sealing of the fuselage against pressurisation loads, while on the wings, which carried all the fuel in integral tanks, there would be the ultimate in fuel-tightness. This was vital, as about 40% of the Comet's total weight at take-off would be fuel.

The basic procedure with Redux was that the resin was applied first and then sprinkled with the plastic powder, and bonding was effected by the application of about 200lb/sq in pressure for 15–20min at a temperature of 145°C.

In the case of the Comet structure, one of the main challenges lay in developing special tools for applying the necessary heat and pressure to compound-curvature panels, such as in the forward fuselage. This required left- and right-handed tools for each stringer for an even pressure to be applied over the whole surface, and it was vital that the mating surfaces of the top and bottom tools were 100%. To

handle all Reduxing operations on the Comet, a total of 64 pairs of tools were produced.

Some of these presses were massive and without precedent, such as the 35ft press for the wing skins and two 25ft double-curvature ones for attaching fuselage stringers to the skin. This comprised top and bottom pressure bars with loose cappings fitted to each bar. The main bars were made from hollow Duralumin extrusions through which steam was circulated to provide the necessary heat.

For the sake of economy, only one set of pressure bars was used, which was formed to the average curvature of the fuselage nose, the cappings being made to accommodate the actual difference.

For this, a plaster model of the nose was made to an accuracy of 1/32in with grooves to represent all the stringers. The variation in curvature between the capping and the actual fuselage was taken up by a casting of low-fusible metal. This was done by offering up the master pressure bar and capping to the plaster model at the required station, blocking the

underside of the gap and pouring the metal into the cavity.

Dovetail grooves in the capping strip ensured that the accurate cast tool-face obtained was firmly keyed to it. The matching tool was made in a similar way by casting against the previously formed face and using graphite to prevent fusion.

ABOVE LEFT Fuselage sections under construction at Hatfield in July 1951. *(Copyright unknown)*

ABOVE A close-up of a window frame in place during construction of a BOAC Comet 1 in February 1951. The Comet's windows are popularly referred to as square, but there was a more generous radius to the corners than is generally realised. *(DH5326C/BAE Systems)*

LEFT The fuselage of G-ALYP out on the Hatfield airfield as work is carried out on the empennage. *(DH4317/BAE Systems)*

LEFT The tailless swept-wing DH108 (VW120) in front of G-ALZK's fuselage on 3 March 1949. Six months earlier, on 6 September 1948, this 108 became the first British aircraft to fly faster than sound in a wild out-of-control dive with John Derry at the controls. *(DH3960E/BAE Systems)*

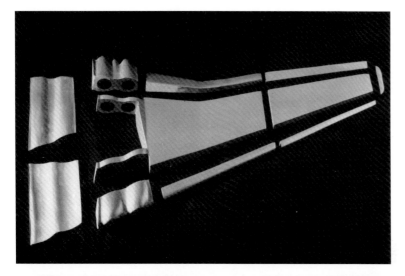

LEFT A crude model showing the main components of the Comet wing. *(DH5340F/BAE Systems)*

CENTRE The drilling jig for the centre section stub-wing. This was built to exacting standards to ensure the extremely accurate drilling of components, as any inaccuracies here would translate into a massive misalignment at the wingtip. Two fitters can be seen working on the wheel well of a production Comet wing in the summer of 1950. Vampires for the Swiss Air Force are under construction in the background. *(Copyright unknown)*

The fuselage side panels consisted of four sheets, 2ft 6in wide by 22ft long, to which all the stringers were Reduxed. These were then joined together internally by lap joints with two single rows of countersunk rivets.

Redux bonding was used extensively on the wing structure, mainly for attaching the stringers to the skin panels. In the inner wing the dog-leg diaphragm spar of the wheel well had its angle-section booms Reduxed to the sheet web, which was itself stiffened with vertical members Reduxed in place.

Among the many other applications of Redux on the Comet was the mounting of the window frames, which were deep-drawn drop-hammer pressings. They were fitted while the fuselage skin was being assembled in the side jig, and two castings were involved in the procedure. One was located in the side jig in the position of the window frame, while the other, which mated with it, was a steam box for applying the correct heat for the adhesive. Steam was fed from a pipe over the top of the jig and the exhaust passed out through steam traps at the bottom. Pressure was exerted by two Mosquito flap-operating jacks, and the whole assembly was mounted on a trolley which could be wheeled into position to any location on the jig. A complete window installation took about 25min, so this was quite a lengthy procedure. However,

LEFT Construction work on the stub-wing halves in March 1950, showing detail of the ribs, spars and wheel well. The four fuselages belong to G-ALYR, YS, ZK and YP. *(DH4597A/BAE Systems)*

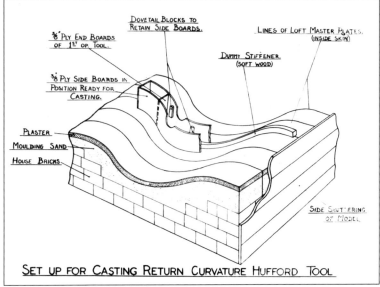

ABOVE Engine intake nacelles in the foreground, while to the rear are the tailpipe assemblies. *(DH5318E/BAE Systems)*

ABOVE RIGHT The elegance of the Comet's graceful air intake nacelles are well shown in this picture *(DH5279B/BAE Systems)*

RIGHT The engine nacelle frame tool. de Havilland used many ingenious money-saving but extremely accurate and effective methods for constructing their own tools. *(DH5098C/BAE Systems)*

on the production aircraft the window cut-out reinforcing plates were punch-riveted as there were difficulties with the Redux operation, and this was to have far-reaching consequences that were not foreseen.

Fuselage assembly

The whole of the floor area for building the fuselage was a vast surface table on which rails were mounted, similar in principle to wartime Mosquito production. The jigs for the various fuselage components were designed as mobile trolleys each fitted with four track-wheels

RIGHT The compound curves of the nacelles were complex and called for specialised tooling. This is the reverse curvature tool for the Comet 1. *(DH5030D/BAE Systems)*

ABOVE A group of visitors to de Havilland in September 1950 is shown details of the Ghost engine. In the background construction work continues on **G-ALYR and YS.** *(DH4994B/BAE Systems)*

ABOVE RIGHT The stub-wing of G-ALYY lined up on the centre section drilling rig. *(DH5287Q/RAE Systems)*

RIGHT A pair of leading edge assemblies. Extreme accuracy was necessary here, and they were built within a tolerance of a hundredth of an inch. *(DH5303H/BAE Systems)*

BELOW A fitter at work on the starboard wing of G-ALYR) in December 1950. In the background is the second prototype (G-ALZK) in the latter stages of assembly. *(Copyright unknown)*

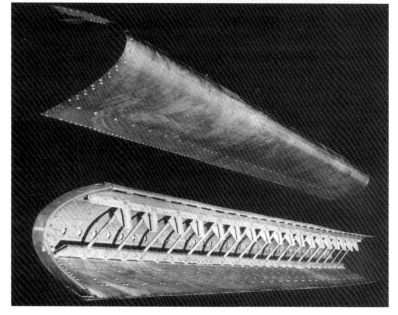

BELOW A diagram of the wing skin and rib attachment tool for the Comet 1. *(DH5305B/BAE Systems)*

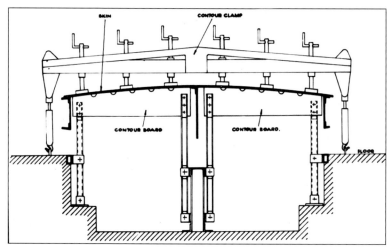

so that once they had received the fuselage sub-assemblies they could be transported to any station for further operations and fitments until the whole fuselage was built up as a complete unit. The fuselage sections comprised the nose, canopy, forward and centre sections, front and rear keels, rear sides, pressure dome and rear cone.

The trolleys were each fitted with V-blocks and surface pads which corresponded with, and could be mated to, any of the surface-plate tools on the line, so that components at the various assembly stations could be accurately lined up with the structure on the trolley.

As with wartime Mosquito assembly, the rails did not have costly and complex turntables for the trolleys to make a right-angle turn, but used the simpler and equally effective method of turning the wheels through 90° on to square steel plates which joined one track to another.

Centre section

A most critical part of the assembly operation was the accurate alignment of the stub-wing centre section with the fuselage; the slightest inaccuracy here would translate into a massive misalignment at the wingtip, and the geometry of the whole aircraft would be hopelessly out of true. This part of the wing was also an integral fuel tank, so great accuracy was also necessary for the mating components to line up, and the operation called for the drilling and reaming of 252 tight-limit holes to attach the stub-wing. This section of the wing had a greater span than the word 'stub' implies, for it extended to the outer edge of the flaps. The outer section would be fitted later.

A large jig was constructed to control the drilling of the nests of holes in top and bottom wing boom attachments of the front and rear spars to the fuselage centre section. These nests were also located in strict relation to each other about the centreline of the fuselage longitudinally and laterally. Two special radial drilling machines were used, with drill heads that could revolve through 360° and operate at any compound angle.

With these machines, jig-drilling could be done vertically downwards through the top spar booms and centre-section fishplates, and by

LEFT The visitors are shown the engine bay of G-ALYR shortly before a Ghost engine is installed. (DH4994D/BAE Systems)

LEFT The second Ghost engine about to be installed on G-ALYP on 29 June 1950. The first engine is already in place. (DH4883/BAE Systems)

BELOW Number one engine about to be installed in the Comet prototype (G-5-1) on 24 March 1949. (DH4004G/BAE Systems)

RIGHT The tailpipe nacelles of the port wing of G-ALYW, photographed on 2 February 1951. The Sprite rocket nacelle is also clearly seen, but this was never used on production aircraft and a pointed tailcone was fitted. This aircraft was delivered to BOAC on 14 June 1952. *(DH5293D/BAE Systems)*

rotating them through 180° the operation could be repeated upwards through the bottom spar booms. In preparation for the drilling operation the wing section was checked for sweep-back, angle of incidence and dihedral.

Before final assembly the stub-wings were taken outside the shop floor on a track trolley for a fluid test to be carried out. Each stub-wing was filled with 2,000gal of paraffin and any weeps were rectified. Although the internal sealing of the tank was made with a rubber seal, the interior was also given a thin coating of Bostik solution as belt-and-braces protection.

The combination of a confined space and toxic fumes made this a hazardous operation, and special protective clothing had to be worn with the provision of a constant supply of fresh air. The suit was fitted with an intercom telephone so that the fitter was in constant touch with those on the outside.

After the fluid test the stub-wing was wheeled on to several track stations for various components to be fitted before finally being mated with the fuselage. Precise alignment with the centreline of the fuselage was achieved with plumb bobs and index plates on the floor, and any adjustment was made with shims. This method proved to be very accurate, and when measurements were taken between each wingtip and fuselage rear cone the difference was only ⁴⁄₁₀in.

All jig trolleys, apart from that supporting the centre section, were then removed and, after a brief 2lb/sq in pressure test was performed, the whole fuselage and stub-wing assembly was wheeled out on to the aerodrome. Well away from the shop floor, where a hull burst would have had horrific consequences, a further test of 11lb/sq in was carried out.

Wing construction

The wing had a 20° sweep-back at quarter chord, but the trailing edge was 'cranked' and swept only on the outer part. For the inner section, the depth required to bury the engines as far as possible within the wing profile while still maintaining a thin airfoil meant an increase

BELOW The Sprite tailcone in place on Comet 1XB. (XM823). *(Philip J. Birtles collection)*

in chord. The result was that the trailing edge of the inner part of the wing was swept forward.

Design, construction and tooling for this area presented some challenges, not only internally for housing the engines while maintaining structural strength, but also for the complex curvatures of the cowls and air intakes. A large number of Hufford stretcher-press tools were required for making the cross-members in the engine cowling, and it was decided for the first time to develop concrete tools.

The method was to cast direct on to the same master model which was used for making the longitudinal skin. All cross-member tools were cast transversely on this model at whatever position they were located. This ensured accuracy of fit and enabled 25 pairs of tools per week to be built by eight men. A total of 195 tools were required for the upper and lower cowls.

After the concrete stretcher-press and Hufford tools had been made from the master model, it was dismantled, and the eight units were used for the manufacture of assembly jigs for the cowling doors. This was done by adding wooden facing strips to the ⅛in-thick metal loft plates and providing hinge locations and trim lines.

The fact that all the stretcher-press tools were taken from the same mould formed by these plates meant that the skins and cross-members made by the tools all fitted accurately on to the assembly jig without the need for any adjustment.

Another complex area of the wing was the wheel well. The undercarriage leg pivoted

ABOVE LEFT Main gear assembly for G-ALYP. The Comet was the first airliner to use a four-wheel bogie-type undercarriage, which was safer and more elegant than the giant single wheel of the prototypes. *(DH5021F/BAE Systems)*

ABOVE The airframe of G-ALYP under construction on 30 November 1950. This aircraft was to become the world's first jet airliner to carry fare-paying passengers when it took off from London Airport on 2 May 1952. In front of YP is the second production Comet (G-ALYR) at a similar stage of construction. *(Crown copyright)*

BELOW Fibreglass proved the best solution to the construction of the many small and complex components for the Comet, and it had the advantage of being stable under extremes of temperature. *(DH5307B/BAE Systems)*

RIGHT A gleaming beauty. The first Comet prototype (G-5-1) nears completion on 2 May 1949. It took to the air for the first time on 27 July that year. *(DH4072A/BAE Systems)*

just outboard of the engine bay and retracted outwards, but the well itself involved multi-angles across the wing, and Redux was used extensively for attaching these angles to the web, with final accuracy being achieved with a rotary miller when the assembly was on its jig.

Wing assembly itself was carried out on similar lines to the fuselage, with sections being built on jigs and moved around on the track, where there were stations for stub-wing drilling, fuel tests, engine cowling attachment, installing ailerons and flaps, and fitting the leading edge.

The first jig was used to locate spars, ribs, wheel-well walls and lower skins on the stub-wing, after which the unit was transferred to the next jig and turned over for attaching the upper skin. Here, the lower skin, which had only been

RIGHT G-ALYW in the latter stages of assembly during March 1952. *(DH6168D/BAE Systems)*

BELOW Production of the Comet 2 at the Chester factory on 14 July 1953. All work ceased after the two Comet 1 tragedies early in 1954. *(DH7205/BAE Systems)*

RIGHT Booster control alignment jig for the Comet Series 2. The Lockheed Servodyne is on the upper right of the picture. *(DH6847E/BAE Systems)*

CENTRE Passenger cabin window jigs for the Comet 2 pictured on 12 February 1953. Eleven months later came the disaster of G-ALYP, and the subsequent accident investigation turned the spotlight on the inherent weaknesses of the window shape. *(DH6828K/BAE Systems)*

located, was removed so that work could be completed inside the wing. It underwent final attachment during the drilling operations, and this meant that no time was wasted between operations on the first two jigs.

A critical component on any wing is the leading edge, and in the case of the Comet this had to be produced to an accuracy of $\frac{1}{100}$in. This was a challenge, but once again was solved by making special tools. These were spar-milled to the correct limits and the 12 SWG metal leading edge sheets were formed by using an Erco stretcher-press, the leading edge material being DTD 710, an aluminium alloy with good stress resistance.

The outer section of each wing was constructed in a similar way to the stub-wing, but was considerably less complex. Upper and lower skins were Reduxed to the stringers on a jig, and this procedure was also followed on the tailplane and fin.

Many assembly operations were carried out from pits so that fitters had easy and comfortable access. The final stages consisted of engine and undercarriage installation; fitting, coupling and testing of ailerons, elevators, rudder, flaps, air brakes and other controls followed by a final inspection. Then the basic aircraft was ready to fly.

The whole construction process illustrates the ingenuity and teamwork that went into the Comet, and how time and money were saved without sacrificing quality.

On production machines the cabin would be fitted out with carpeting, seating and many other features, for the safety and comfort of passengers who would experience the kind of luxurious travel envisaged in the brave and exciting new world of jet airliners.

LEFT The final stages – and a steady hand required. A de Havilland sign writer paints the words that say it all on the nose of the first prototype. *(DH4208C/BAE Systems)*

Chapter Three

Comet
anatomy

—⟨●⟩——————————

The Comet was more conventional
than its graceful lines, jet engines
and prodigious performance
would suggest, but it had a
number of safety and operational
systems that have remained
standard on airliners to this day.
The passenger cabin was the
epitome of taste and luxury and
a far cry from today's more basic
budget travel.

OPPOSITE **A good view of the radar installation in the nose of
Comet 4 G-APDF.** *(DH11719D/BAE Systems)*

General description

BELOW A cutaway model of the first Comet prototype (G-ALVG) showing the passenger seating layout, galley immediately behind the flight deck, and the ladies' and gentlemen's dressing rooms. *(Airspeed 028126G/BAE Systems)*

Its unbroken purity of line gave the Comet 1 a futuristic appearance, but the overall external layout was relatively orthodox – although extensive measures were taken with the airframe to keep weight as low as possible while being consistent with strength and safety. It was a low-wing cantilever monoplane with mildly swept-back wings and conventional tailplane and fin. With seating for 44 passengers, it was powered by four de Havilland Ghost 50 jet engines housed in the wing roots, and was designed to cruise at 460mph at altitudes of up to 42,000ft to maximise economy of the fuel-thirsty jets.

The tailplane had no sweep-back, but a pronounced dihedral to keep it clear of the jet efflux, and the fin and rudder were smaller than many piston engine airliners of the era. The undercarriage on production machines was a four-wheel bogie type under each wing and power-assisted steerable twin nose wheels.

As many components as possible were interchangeable for ease of production and to minimise time and costs. The same engines, tailplanes, elevators and brakes could be fitted on either side of the aircraft with no modifications.

Fuselage

The fuselage constructed from aluminium alloy was of circular section 10ft 3in wide, comprising the nose, canopy, forward section, sides, front and rear keel, rear sides, pressure dome and rear conc. The nose had a compound curvature with a slightly drooping centreline that incorporated the cockpit glazing. Passenger windows were square with radiused corners and entry to the seating area was via an inward-opening door at the rear on the port

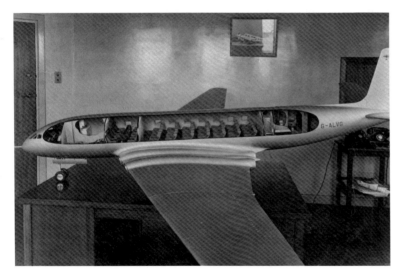

BELOW Scale drawings of the Comet 1 showing seating arrangements, equipment bay, freight compartment, access doors and crew locations. *(Copyright unknown)*

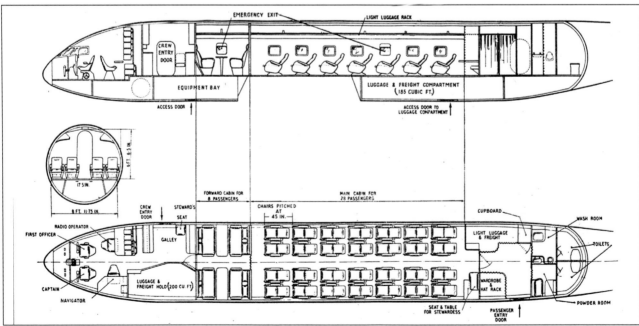

side. Two emergency exit hatches were on each side of the fuselage – two in the forward cabin area and two in the main seating area by the fourth row of seats from the rear. Crew entrance was on the starboard side of the forward fuselage. All hydraulic cables, pipes, electrical wiring and other equipment were installed under the cabin floor and easily accessible through hatches on the underside of the fuselage.

The aesthetically satisfying beauty of the Comet was complemented by the passenger cabin's carefully selected fixtures and fittings that combined functionality with luxury. Restraint and taste were the order of the day. On entering the aircraft, passengers would step into a spacious foyer floored with dark blue wool pile carpet. Immediately to the left was a royal blue curtained wardrobe with a hat rack, while opposite was a stowage area for light luggage with similar curtains. Behind this was a radio and 'official stowage' department, with a door panelled in weathered sycamore veneer beneath a plastic surface.

The rear wall of the entry foyer was also panelled in plastic-finished sycamore, and a central pier containing a silver-anodised drum-type ash canister with the BOAC badge above it was flanked by royal blue curtained doorways. These led into the women's (port) and men's (starboard) dressing rooms – or 'ladies' and 'gentlemen' as they were in the days before the genders were depicted with symbols.

The two compartments were similar, the differences being in detail and colour. The floor of the ladies' room was fitted with deep-pile smoky-grey nylon carpet, which contrasted with the delicate pink of the furnishings and the grey of the leather-cloth walls and ceiling. Above the pink washbasin was a recess in the inboard wall for a large mirror with a ring-tray flanked by box compartments for face tissues. Against the outboard wall, and facing to the rear, was a fixed seat for the fitted dressing table with bottles of lotions and creams at the foot of a 20in by18in mirror.

Facilities were a little less elaborate for the men, but their dressing room was described at the time as 'striking a nice balance between masculinity and the sybaritic'. Walls and ceiling were covered in grey Vynide, the floor in dark blue PVC and the washbasin was in silver-anodised light alloy. Above the basin was a beige-grey moulded plastic fitting incorporating a tray and boxes for paper tissues, while beneath the basin were drawers and cabinets for towels.

To the rear of the basin was a dressing table with receptacles for shaving lotion, talcum powder, and hair lotion. Beneath the table was a recess and below that a cupboard. All these fittings were also in beige-grey plastic. A 14in by 9in bracket-hinged mirror was set at an angle

BELOW Artwork showing the layout and tastefully understated decor of the Comet 1 passenger cabin. *(Flight)*

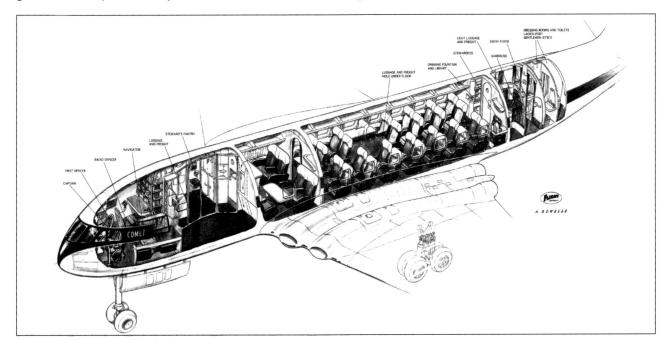

RIGHT An artist's portrayal of some of the Comet's fittings and fixtures: the galley (left), forward passenger cabin and main passenger cabin. Comfort and luxury was the order of the day. (Flight)

just inside the doorway, and a power socket was provided for electric razors.

Each dressing room had a separate compartment fitted with a self-flushing Vickers toilet.

From the entry foyer, passengers went through a bulkhead door into the main cabin, where immediately to the left was a small but well-equipped station for the steward or stewardess. On the right was a filtered drinking water dispenser, and, as a nod to the old steamship days, 'the ship's library'.

The main cabin area was 39ft 9½in long, and the standard BOAC version seated 28 passengers in seven rows (or 36 in nine rows as an alternative for shorter-stage flights), while the

forward cabin was 7ft long and accommodated a further eight passengers in four double seats that faced each other.

A central aisle 17½in wide divided the rows of armchairs, which were BOAC 'Overseas' Mk 33 reclining units by Vickers with foldaway tables in the back plus the usual pockets and lifebelt stowage. Upholstered in foam rubber and covered in a herringbone-weave blue and wool-faced tapestry, they were described in Flight magazine as 'sumptuous receivers of the human body'. Each seat position had an individual reading light and steward call button developed specifically for the Comet by the Walters Electrical Manufacturing Company of London, while gangway lights were fitted at floor level.

At each of the seats, which could recline from 17° to 45° (or 39° in the 44-passenger layout), was a window set in a splayed surround of beige-grey plastic and curtained with wavy candy-striped linen in Indian red and white. As in the foyer, the floor was covered in deep-pile dark blue carpet, which extended up the base of the side walls to form a wainscot where the air-entry ducts for the cabin conditioning were situated.

On Comets with extra passenger capacity there was a small reduction in light luggage space, so the steward's or stewardess's desk at the rear had to go.

The walls and ceiling were finished in a cool grey shade of leather-cloth formed in flat panels running the length of the cabin, which took away the feeling for passengers that they were sitting in a tube. The overhead racks for light luggage also helped to break up the circumference.

The forward end of the main cabin ended with a structural bulkhead. On the other side of this was a more intimate eight-seat passenger compartment. This had fixed chairs in facing

WINDOWS

de Havilland had made an early decision to use single window panes for the pilots' direct-vision panels and for the small circular windows in the entrance doors. Although the CAA (Civil Aviation Authority) did not agree with this practice, de Havilland felt that as long as the windows were properly designed and stressed, two panes were no better than one.

However, all other windows were double-thickness units, the layers being a thin, unstressed sheet of Perspex on the inside which could withstand the great temperature difference between the interior and exterior air, a gap supplied with dry air from a desiccator, and an outer thick sheet of Perspex to carry the pressure difference.

An exception to this was in the case of the windscreen panels directly in front of the pilots, which had a thick pressure-resisting pane on the inside and a sheet of laminated glass on the outside.

Four of the passenger windows formed emergency exits above the wing, and could be released from inside or outside the aircraft. As with all other doors and hatches, they opened inwards so that no inadvertent release of air was possible.

pairs with a removable Wareite plastic veneer-topped table between them. Wareite was the forerunner of Formica and was produced at a factory in Ware, Hertfordshire.

The doorway in the forward end wall of this cabin was fitted with a base-hinged flap which could be lowered to form a server table, so that the steward could pass food and drink through from the galley to the stewardess in the cabin without having to continually open the main door. In those days all food was served individually and there was no trolley wheeled down the central aisle.

The galley itself occupied approximately half the width of the fuselage, but was spacious and equipped with a GEC electric oven that would heat meals for 12 passengers in 10–12min from frozen. A pre-set time switch rang a warning bell at the end of the heating period. The oven operated at 28 volts DC and was loaded at 3kW, with a 1kW frying unit at the bottom. Cabinets and storage cupboards were finished in brightly buffed Alclad aluminium, and a tip-up steward's seat was located on the starboard side. Most of the meals were provided by the food giant J. Lyons, while custom plastic crockery was designed and made by British Artid Plastic Ltd.

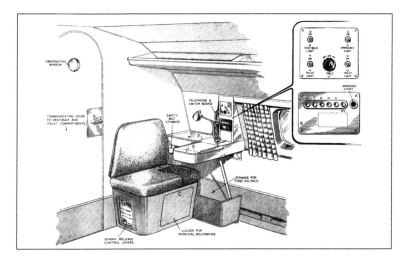

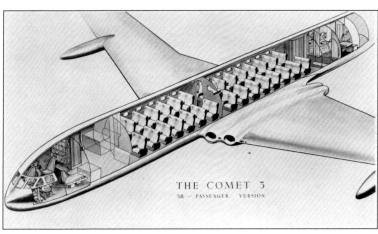

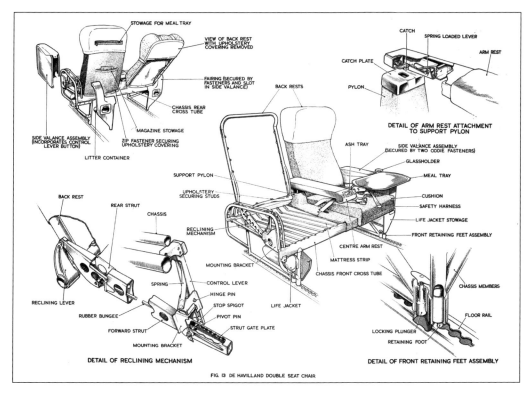

FIG. 13 DE HAVILLAND DOUBLE SEAT CHAIR

TOP The stewardess's station on the Comet 1. (www.flight-manuals-on-cd.com)

ABOVE A cutaway of the Comet 3 cabin. The layout was very similar to that of the Comet 1, the main difference being that it could accommodate about twice the number of passengers. (DH6754H/BAE Systems)

LEFT Diagram of the seating for the Comet 3, which was used for development work on the Comet 4. (DH8174A/BAE Systems)

de Havilland Comet 1. *(Mike Badrocke)*

1 Nose cone
2 Nose construction
3 Windscreen frame panel
4 Instrument panel shroud
5 Rudder pedals
6 Windscreen wiper
7 Cockpit roof construction
8 Co-pilot's seat
9 Control column
10 Pilot's seat
11 Engineer's control panel
12 Swivelling engineer's seat
13 Navigator's seat
14 Navigator's worktable
15 Nosewheel bay construction
16 Nose undercarriage leg
17 Twin nosewheels
18 Nosewheel door
19 HF grid aerial
20 Navigational instrument rack
21 Engineer's work table
22 Radio and electrical rack
23 Observation window
24 Crew's wardrobe and locker
25 Crew entry door
26 Forward luggage and freight hold
27 Hydraulic equipment bay
28 Control cable runs
29 Maintenance access hatch
30 Ice inspection window
31 Galley
32 Aft-facing seats (one row)
33 ADF loop aerials
34 Dining table
35 Smoke room seating (eight passengers)
36 Emergency escape window
37 Air conditioning plant
38 Air conditioning distribution duct
39 Partition door to main cabin
40 Starboard inner wing fuel tanks
41 Outer wing fuel tanks
42 Leading edge wing fence
43 Pitot tube

44 Starboard navigation light
45 Static discharge wicks
46 Starboard aileron
47 Aileron tab
48 Flap outer section
49 Airbrake (upper and lower surfaces)
50 Fuel jettison pipe
51 Flap inboard section
52 Undercarriage bay upper panel
53 Fuselage frame construction
54 Cabin floor construction
55 Wing centre-section fuel tank bays
56 Window frame panels
57 Fuselage main frame
58 Aft luggage and freight hold
59 Floor beam construction
60 Air conditioning outlet vents
61 Cabin trim panels
62 Overhead coat rack
63 Main cabin seating (36 passengers)
64 Emergency escape window
65 Luggage and freight hold loading door
66 Drinking water fountain
67 Book and magazine rack
68 Aft cabin door
69 Wardrobe
70 Official stowage locker
71 Aft radio rack
72 Toilet compartment partition with curtained doors
73 Ladies powder room/wash room
74 Toilet
75 Rear pressure dome

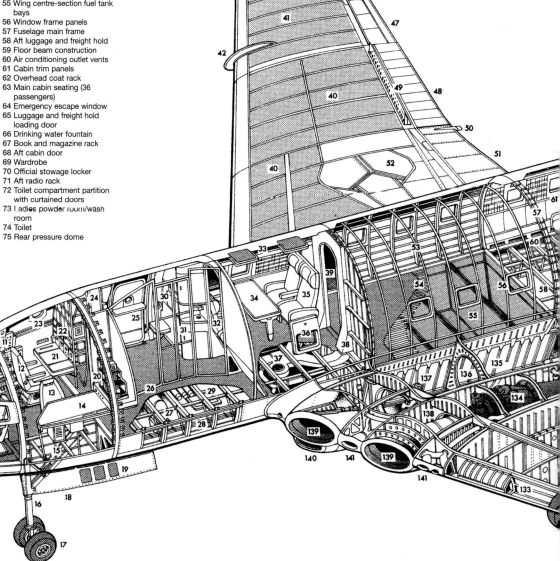

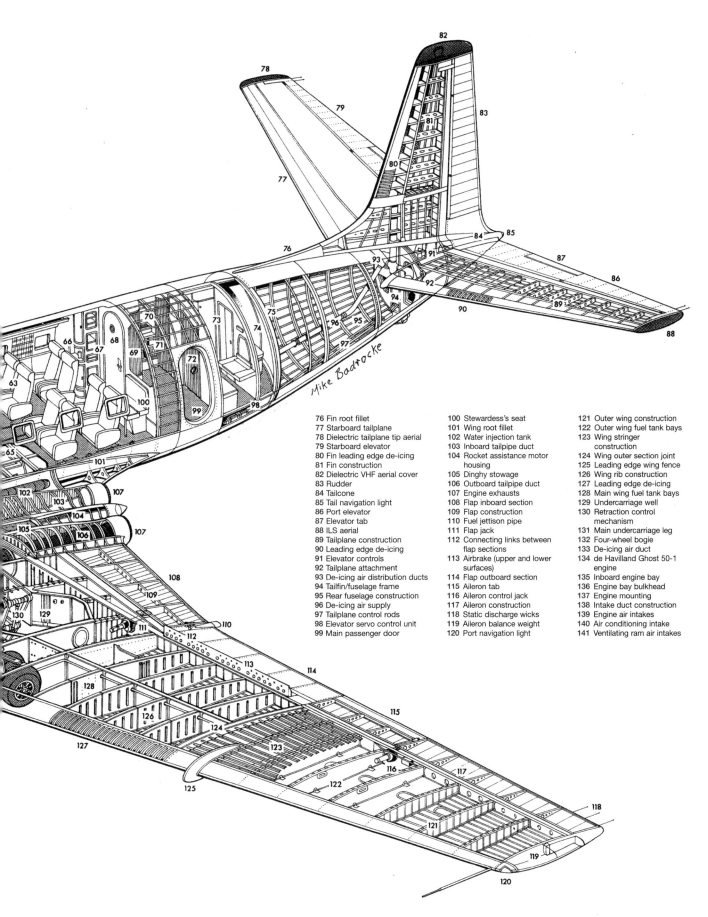

76 Fin root fillet
77 Starboard tailplane
78 Dielectric tailplane tip aerial
79 Starboard elevator
80 Fin leading edge de-icing
81 Fin construction
82 Dielectric VHF aerial cover
83 Rudder
84 Tailcone
85 Tail navigation light
86 Port elevator
87 Elevator tab
88 ILS aerial
89 Tailplane construction
90 Leading edge de-icing
91 Elevator controls
92 Tailplane attachment
93 De-icing air distribution ducts
94 Tailfin/fuselage frame
95 Rear fuselage construction
96 De-icing air supply
97 Tailplane control rods
98 Elevator servo control unit
99 Main passenger door

100 Stewardess's seat
101 Wing root fillet
102 Water injection tank
103 Inboard tailpipe duct
104 Rocket assistance motor
housing
105 Dinghy stowage
106 Outboard tailpipe duct
107 Engine exhausts
108 Flap inboard section
109 Flap construction
110 Fuel jettison pipe
111 Flap jack
112 Connecting links between
flap sections
113 Airbrake (upper and lower
surfaces)
114 Flap outboard section
115 Aileron tab
116 Aileron control jack
117 Aileron construction
118 Static discharge wicks
119 Aileron balance weight
120 Port navigation light

121 Outer wing construction
122 Outer wing fuel tank bays
123 Wing stringer
construction
124 Wing outer section joint
125 Leading edge wing fence
126 Wing rib construction
127 Leading edge de-icing
128 Main wing fuel tank bays
129 Undercarriage well
130 Retraction control
mechanism
131 Main undercarriage leg
132 Four-wheel bogie
133 De-icing air duct
134 de Havilland Ghost 50-1
engine
135 Inboard engine bay
136 Engine bay bulkhead
137 Engine mounting
138 Intake duct construction
139 Engine air intakes
140 Air conditioning intake
141 Ventilating ram air intakes

ART OF THE CUTAWAY

When it comes to the perspective cutaway, no one does it better than Mike Badrocke. With a portfolio showing the detailed anatomy of 640 different types of aircraft, he still gets requests for new drawings.

Mike joined the de Havilland Aircraft Company as an apprentice and worked in the wing and fuselage shops of the Comet 4 in 1958–59, so gained plenty of first-hand knowledge of how aircraft are put together. After developing his talent for technical artwork, he left de Havilland in 1963 to work for *Flight* and later *Aircraft International*, where his name became synonymous with the definitive cutaway.

There is no quick route to preparing a perspective cutaway; it involves diligent research down to the finest detail, and then the talent to produce it as a three-dimensional presentation.

For the last 40 years Mike has worked freelance, and his art is in constant demand for many aviation publications – including, of course, this one.

RIGHT Mike Badrocke. *(Courtesy Mike Badrocke)*

Opposite the galley and immediately in front of the eight-seat cabin was a 200cu ft freight and luggage hold, while a further under-floor storage area of 185cu ft was located at the rear of the main cabin. Access to this was by a door on the underside of the fuselage. This was not popular with baggage handlers, as every piece of luggage had to be loaded vertically upwards from the baggage truck and then slid along the floor to be stacked. It was laborious and time-consuming.

The flight deck

Although crew duties could be varied to some extent by different operators, and to handle different radio facilities, the basic layout of the Comet's flight deck was developed

BELOW The galley panel. *(www.flight-manuals-on-cd.com)*

RIGHT Comet 1 engine controls and instruments. *(www.flight-manuals-on-cd.com)*

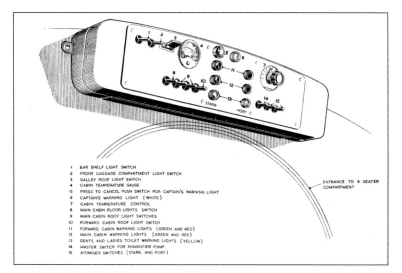

1 BAR SHELF LIGHT SWITCH
2 FRONT LUGGAGE COMPARTMENT LIGHT SWITCH
3 GALLEY ROOF LIGHT SWITCH
4 CABIN TEMPERATURE GAUGE
5 PRESS TO CANCEL PUSH SWITCH FOR CAPTAIN'S WARNING LIGHT
6 CAPTAIN'S WARNING LIGHT (WHITE)
7 CABIN TEMPERATURE CONTROL
8 MAIN CABIN FLOOR LIGHTS SWITCH
9 MAIN CABIN ROOF LIGHT SWITCHES
10 FORWARD CABIN ROOF LIGHT SWITCH
11 FORWARD CABIN WARNING LIGHTS (GREEN AND RED)
12 MAIN CABIN WARNING LIGHTS (GREEN AND RED)
13 GENTS AND LADIES TOILET WARNING LIGHTS (YELLOW)
14 MASTER SWITCH FOR HUMIDIFIER PUMP
15 ATOMISER SWITCHES (STARB. AND PORT)

ENTRANCE TO 8 SEATER COMPARTMENT

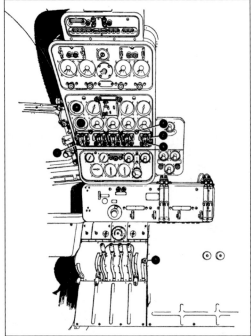

and standardised after many discussions – particularly with BOAC, who were the first purchasers and operators – and it was not thought that anything other than minor modifications would need to be done by other airlines. The layout was similar to that of the Lockheed Constellation, an aircraft that was popular with BOAC passengers and crews.

There were four main instrument and equipment groups, which were logically laid out for the duties involved:

1   Primary instruments and controls, including the two standard duplicated flight panels, for the captain and first officer.
2   Engineering panels and controls on the starboard side.
3   Equipment and navigator's station on the port side.

ABOVE The Comet 1 flight crew at work. The first officer's seat could swivel and slide back, and here he can be seen attending to the engineer's panel. On the left behind the pilot is the navigator. *(DH6703A/BAE Systems)*

BELOW The flight deck of a Comet 1, photographed in October 1951. The engineer's station is behind the first officer's seat on the right, while the navigator would be behind the captain. *(DH5828A/BAE Systems)*

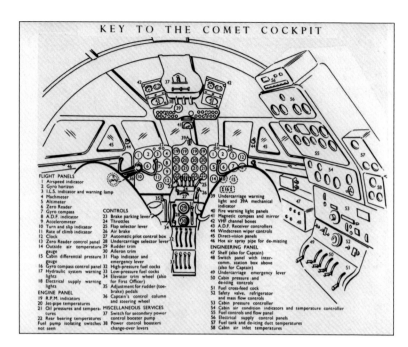

KEY TO THE COMET COCKPIT

FLIGHT PANELS
1 Airspeed indicator
2 Gyro horizon
3 I.L.S. indicator and warning lamp
4 Machmeter
5 Altimeter
6 Zero Reader
7 Gyro compass
8 A.D.F. indicator
9 Accelerometer
10 Turn and slip indicator
11 Rate of climb indicator
12 Clock
13 Zero Reader control panel
14 Outside air temperature gauge
15 Cabin differential pressure gauge
16 Gyro compass control panel
17 Hydraulic system warning lights
18 Electrical supply warning lights

ENGINE PANEL
19 R.P.M. indicators
20 Jet-pipe temperatures
21 Oil pressures and temperatures
22 Rear bearing temperatures
23 Fuel pump isolating switches not seen

CONTROLS
23 Brake parking lever
24 Throttles
25 Flap selector lever
26 Air brake
27 Automatic pilot control box
28 Undercarriage selector lever
29 Rudder trim
30 Aileron trim
31 Flap indicator and emergency lever
32 High-pressure fuel cocks
33 Low-pressure fuel cocks
34 Elevator trim wheel (also for First Officer)
35 Adjustment for rudder (toe-brake) pedals
36 Captain's control column and steering wheel

MISCELLANEOUS SERVICES
37 Switch for secondary power control booster pump
38 Power control boosters change-over levers

39 Undercarriage warning light and 39A mechanical indicator
40 Fire warning light panels
41 Magnetic compass and mirror
42 VHF channel boxes
43 A.D.F. Receiver controllers
44 Windscreen wiper controls
45 Direct-vision panels
46 Hot air spray pipe for de-misting

ENGINEERING PANEL
47 Shelf (also for Captain)
48 Switch panel with inter-comm. station box above (also for Captain)
49 Undercarriage emergency lever
50 Cabin pressure and de-icing controls
51 Fuel cross-feed cock
52 Safety valve, refrigerator
53 Cabin pressure controller
54 Cabin air condition indicators and temperature controller
55 Fuel controls and flow panel
56 Electrical supply control panels
57 Fuel tank and de-icing duct temperatures
58 Cabin air inlet temperatures

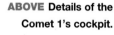 **ABOVE Details of the Comet 1's cockpit.** *(www.flight-manuals-on-cd.com)*

ABOVE The captain's control column and instrument panel. This is the first prototype on 21 May 1951, by which time it had clocked up many hours and acquired some paint chips and scuffing on the column. *(DH5510B/BAE Systems)*

4 Radio operator's equipment and table on the starboard side.

Both pilots' seats were adjustable for tilt and height, and could also slide backwards 16in as well as being able to swivel 60° outboard and 30° inboard. This would enable the first officer to reach the engineer's panel if necessary.

The primary instrument panel for the engines and the control pedestal, which carried engine, trimming, undercarriage and flap controls, plus the main fuel pressure cocks, was mounted centrally between the two pilots, each of whom had a panel carrying the main instruments.

Nose-wheel steering was operated solely by the captain with a hand wheel at the elbow of the cranked control column, and the wheel brakes were controlled differentially by toe pedals on the rudder controls. The parking brake was on the main central pedestal.

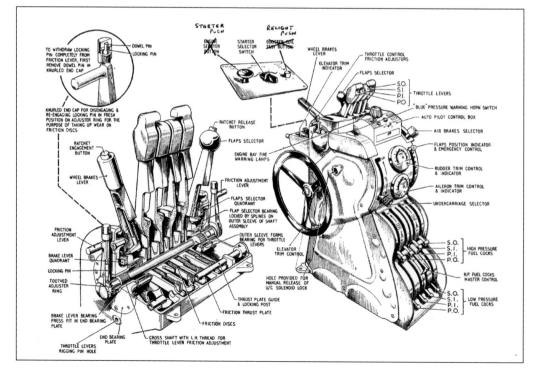

RIGHT The control pedestal in the Comet 1. *(www.flight-manuals-on-cd.com)*

In the roof above the centre of the windscreen were duplicated 70-channel VHF selector boxes, Marconi ADF (Automatic Direction Finder) Type AD 7092B and emergency flying control change-over levers. Immediately above the screen, forward of the roof panel and easily seen, was a separate panel containing emergency warning lights and fire control buttons.

Controls for the Smiths SEP 1 automatic pilot were on the central control pedestal, and in addition to the Sperry CL2 gyro-compass dials in the flight panels, a magnetic compass was centrally placed above the windscreen.

The most important new instrument was the Sperry Zero Reader; the Comet was the first British commercial aircraft to have this fitted. Its 'brain' was an electronic and mathematical flight computer which correlated information from the gyro-compass, altimeter, artificial horizon and the cross-pointer ILS (Instrument Landing System) indicator. This presented the pilot with a unified picture so that he could hold the aircraft on the optimum flight path during complex procedures.

The engineer's panel housed controls and instruments for the Comet's ancillary systems and instruments for the fuel supply. In the centre were the fuel capacity and fuel-flow gauges with

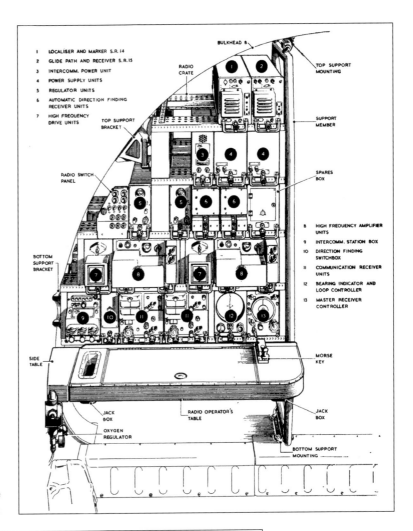

1   LOCALISER AND MARKER S.R.14
2   GLIDE PATH AND RECEIVER S.R.15
3   INTERCOMM. POWER UNIT
4   POWER SUPPLY UNITS
5   REGULATOR UNITS
6   AUTOMATIC DIRECTION FINDING RECEIVER UNITS
7   HIGH FREQUENCY DRIVE UNITS
8   HIGH FREQUENCY AMPLIFIER UNITS
9   INTERCOMM. STATION BOX
10 DIRECTION FINDING SWITCHBOX
11 COMMUNICATION RECEIVER UNITS
12 BEARING INDICATOR AND LOOP CONTROLLER
13 MASTER RECEIVER CONTROLLER

ABOVE Comet 1 radio operator's station. *(www.flight-manuals-on-cd.com)*

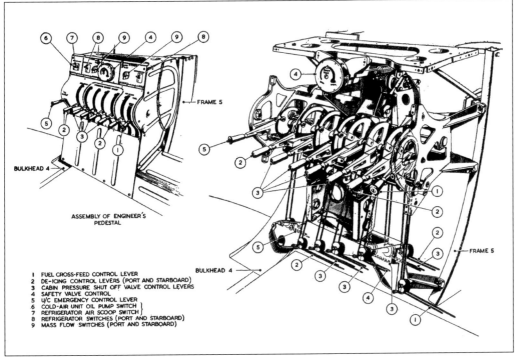

ASSEMBLY OF ENGINEER'S PEDESTAL

1   FUEL CROSS-FEED CONTROL LEVER
2   DE-ICING CONTROL LEVERS (PORT AND STARBOARD)
3   CABIN PRESSURE SHUT OFF VALVE CONTROL LEVERS
4   SAFETY VALVE CONTROL
5   U/C EMERGENCY CONTROL LEVER
6   COLD-AIR UNIT OIL PUMP SWITCH
7   REFRIGERATOR AIR SCOOP SWITCH
8   REFRIGERATOR SWITCHES (PORT AND STARBOARD)
9   MASS FLOW SWITCHES (PORT AND STARBOARD)

LEFT Engineer's pedestal. *(www.flight-manuals-on-cd.com)*

1 HOT CUP SWITCH BOX
2 CUP RACK
3 CROCKERY CRATE
4 FRESH WATER TANK FILLER
5 FRESH WATER TAP
6 FOOD STOWAGE CUPBOARDS
7 OXYGEN CHARGING ACCESS PANEL
8 WASTE BIN
9 HYDRAULIC EMERGENCY HAND PUMP
10 CUTLERY STOWAGE DRAWERS
11 FOLDING TABLE
12 2 GALLON URN
13 URN FILLER TAP
14 FRESH WATER TANK
15 ROOF LAMP
16 VENTILATION GRILLES
17 PANTRY CUPBOARD
18 TELEPHONE AND SWITCH BOARD
19 STAND-BY LIGHT SWITCH
20 ICE FORMATION SPOT-LAMP SWITCH
21 OVEN
22 HOT CUP STOWAGE
23 ICE FORMATION SPOT-LAMP
24 ICE DETECTION WINDOW
25 SAFETY BELT STOWAGE
26 STEWARD'S FOLDING SEAT
27 REFRIGERATOR
28 DRY PROVISIONS CUPBOARD
29 BAR CUPBOARD
30 GLASS STOWAGE CUPBOARD
31 GALLEY PANEL
32 SERVING HATCH
33 COMMUNICATING DOOR TO 8 SEATER COMPARTMENT

the immersion pump switches, while below the panel were the cabin air-conditioning controls and instruments, the pressure controller and the refrigeration control. At the base of the panel were the de-icing controls and main cabin pressure control valves.

The navigator had a swivelling and sliding seat so that he could see other essential instruments and also reach the engineer's panel if necessary. His station was fitted with controls for the No 2 Marconi AD 7092A ADF equipment, which was duplicated for the pilot's and radio operator's use, and the Sperry gyro-compass. In the roof above him was a mounting for a periscope sextant.

The radio operator's seat normally faced rearwards, but, like the navigator's, could also swivel through 360°. His equipment included the duplicated Marconi ADF unit; the HF communications AD107 transmitter, also duplicated; and twin AD 94 HF/MF receivers. Standard Telephones and Cables VHF was used, the set being the STR 12C, again duplicated (70 channels each set). Standard also supplied the SR 14A/15A ILS receiver, and the intercom was by Ultra. Ex-RAF Rebecca/Eureka radio navigation was fitted and used in conjunction with Type 953 ground responder beacons.

Much of the equipment was virtually the same as in BOAC's Canadair Argonauts and Handley Page Hermes, so was well proven. On the Comet the radio installation was served entirely by aerials hidden within the airframe to reduce drag to a minimum.

Wings

The wing was built of light aluminium alloy with conventional spar, rib and stringer construction. Upper and lower skins were Reduxed to the stringers to give a super-clean and smooth surface with minimal drag. The engines were housed in the wing roots between the front and rear main spars, and the fact that the wing was low afforded easy access for engine maintenance, while the absence of propellers meant that the undercarriage legs could be as short as possible.

The underside of the wing in the engine bay area consisted of hinged panels that allowed complete and easy access for maintenance, while further panels were located on the upper surface.

The large split flaps, which extended to the ailerons, were shaped on the underside to blend with the curves of the jet-pipes. Air brakes were fitted to the upper and lower surfaces of the wing immediately in front of the outer part of the flaps, and would compensate for the lack of braking power provided by propellers. No leading edge slats were fitted, but on production aircraft each wing had a single fence to help prevent the boundary layer air flowing outwards at the leading edge – a characteristic of swept wings at low speed and high angles of attack.

The wing served as an integral fuel tank, with the centre section containing 2,020gal in bag tanks, while two inboard tanks each held 785gal and two outboard ones each carried 1,220gal. This totalled 6,030gal in five tank groups for early production Comets for BOAC.

A specially designed Harley 11KDC/1 landing light was housed in each wing about 45ft outboard and set to shine ahead parallel with the line of flight. The lamp was retractable and lay flush with the underside of the wing surface when not in use. Actuation was electrical and it could be moved to any position within 90°. It was fitted with a Harley double filament 750/240W bulb, the higher power being used for take-off and landing. The filaments were automatically extinguished during the final stages of retraction. However, this diffuser type of lamp was not as popular with pilots as sealed beam units, as it could be used for only 5min at a time to prevent overheating and cracking, while the low-

FAR LEFT The control column, instruments and rudder pedal of Comet C2 (XN453), which started life as a Comet 2 (G-AMXD) for BOAC. (DH128990K/ BAE Systems)

LEFT An electrician wiring up systems behind the Comet flight deck. (Copyright unknown)

ABOVE A shot taken from the passenger cabin of G-ALYS, BOAC's first Comet, showing the air brakes deployed on the starboard wing. *(Frank Hudson, Associated Newspapers)*

powered filaments for taxiing were considered almost useless.

Landing gear

Apart from the two prototypes, which had a single large wheel under each wing, the Comet was fitted with a four-wheel bogie-type undercarriage. It was the first aircraft to go into airline service with this configuration, and also the first in service with large light-alloy forgings for the landing gear. The gear was retracted and lowered hydraulically, with a hand pump available for emergencies. Inadvertent retraction on the ground was not possible.

The bogie layout gave a superior ride and better performance on rough surfaces

compared to large single wheels. It was also much safer, as a tyre blow-out would have little effect, whereas a single wheel would prove much more serious.

The main-wheel tyres were Dunlop 35.00 × 17 size and operated at 120lb/sq in at an all-up aircraft weight of 105,000lb. Initially the tyres were ribbed, but this design picked up debris on runways so it was changed to a dimpled tread, which not only cured the problem but was stronger under side-loads.

Brakes were duplicated Dunlop discs, and later much thicker ones were fitted to cope with the heaviest braking without overheating. These could take three machining operations, which trebled their life, and, as there were 16 discs in total, amounted to considerable savings in time and cost.

The nose wheel had powered steering. This was essential, as the Comet could not use differential engine power for ground manoeuvring, unlike piston engine aircraft. Tyre pressure was 70lb/sq in.

Systems

Hydraulics

The Comet's flying control system, undercarriage retraction, flaps, nose-wheel steering, air brakes and wheel brakes were all operated hydraulically from five separate

RIGHT The four-wheel bogie gear that replaced the single wheel on the wing of the prototypes and which was used on all production Comets. *(Copyright unknown)*

FAR RIGHT The steerable nose wheel of the Comet 1. This had to undergo extensive testing on a makeshift truck at Hatfield, as the Comet would not be able to steer on the ground by using differential engine thrust, as is the case with multi-engine propeller aircraft. *(Crown copyright)*

colour-coded circuits. Power was provided by six Lockheed Mk 7 pumps, four of which were driven by the Ghost engines and the other two by battery-operated electric motors. An unusually high degree of back-up was provided, and failure of an engine would not affect the main or booster systems. As long as the Comet had enough power to fly there would always be at least one hydraulic circuit in operation.

The complete system was designed by de Havilland and consisted of the following colour-coded systems:

Green: landing-gear retraction, nose-wheel steering, wheel and air brakes, flaps, flying control secondary servos and windscreen wipers. This circuit was fed by a pump on each outer engine.

Blue: actuation of primary Lockheed Servodyne units for power assistance of flying controls. Blue fluid could not be introduced into any other system, and vice versa. The circuit was connected to a pump on each inner engine.

Yellow: emergency system which took over the secondary servo units in the event of blue and green circuits failing. Power was supplied by an electrically driven pump. The yellow circuit could also be used for ground testing the flying controls when no other power was available.

Red: standby system, which could be used for emergency lowering of the undercarriage and operation of flaps, wheel brakes and steering. Power was supplied from an individual electrically driven pump, and the red supply could be passed through all normal systems, other than the flying control primary servos, for ground testing.

Broken red: manual system with a hand pump to energise the emergency down-lines of the undercarriage only.

The systems were of the constant pressure type with accumulators for additional energy storage. Hydraulic fluid used on early Comets was Lockheed 22, a castor-based oil. Each pump had a flow indicator to give early warning to the crew of any pressure loss, and the systems were individually labelled with their respective colour codes, which made servicing simple and straightforward.

Normal working pressure was 2,500lb/sq in, and the changeover from blue to green for flying control power was assisted by the accumulators, which smoothed the operation of the boosters through secondary pressure lines.

Flying controls

The powered flying control system was basically simple, and there was no manual reversion, but with the multi-duplication of services this was not considered an issue. Elevators and ailerons were operated by dual control columns

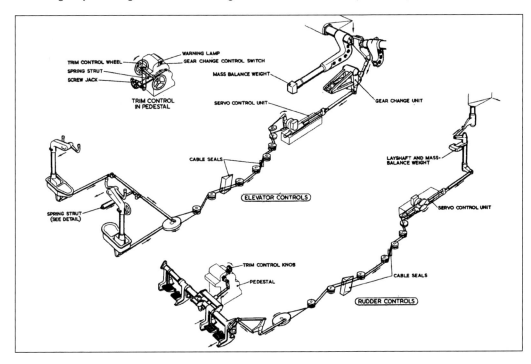

LEFT Flying controls of the Comet 1.
(*www.flight-manuals-on-cd.com*)

fitted with 'W'-type hand wheels. On top of the port column was a steering wheel for the nose wheel, with a white arrow pointing vertically upwards to indicate the neutral setting.

Dual pendulum-type rudder bars were fitted and were independently adjustable for reach. Dual elevator trim wheels and single aileron and rudder trim controls were mounted on the central control pedestal.

The Lockheed Servodynes were grouped near the centre of the aircraft, and two – one of which was in reserve – were dedicated for each flying control. Each pair was mechanically inter-connected by the linkage to the control surface, and, in the case of the elevator and rudder controls, the two were bolted back to back in tandem.

Only one of the Servodynes in any pair was energised, while its companion followed the movement passively. The primary (blue) circuit would normally operate the active unit, but fluid passages could be opened up on this jack to give a free flow so that the passive servo could be energised by the secondary (yellow) circuit. The changeover between the circuits was smooth and imperceptible.

The systems had flow indicators at each pump to warn the pilot of any change in normal delivery, and Purolator micronic filters were able to separate out foreign matter down to five microns in size. Protection against loss of oil owing to a burst hydraulic gauge or a pipe leak was provided by a piece of equipment designed specifically for the Comet by Barnet Instruments Ltd and known as the Comet Transmitter. It was fitted between the pump and the gauge and prevented any sudden loss of fluid under high pressure.

Powered flying controls would take some acclimatising to for a pilot accustomed to cable-and-pulley manual operation: not only were stick forces much lower, but in the case of the Comet's ailerons there was no exponential resistance to give a feel for what was happening, in spite of the many trials carried out on the DH108. Stick force did vary on the Comet's rudder and elevators, but as the former was hardly ever used and most longitudinal control was carried out with the trimmers, this was of little relevance.

Trimming controls consisted of biasing spring struts actuated by screw threads from the central cockpit pedestal. Their effect was very slightly delayed, as they did not act on the surface directly.

Electrics

The main electrical contractor was British Thomson-Houston, who provided four large 8.5kVA three-phase alternators, one of which was mounted on each engine. These supplied AC current which was rectified and paralleled, and the resulting current available was anything up to 220 amps per set. The single-pole electrical system was kept to 28 volts DC by carbon-pile regulators, and auxiliary power was provided by inverter sets driven by DC motors, which delivered supplies of single-phase current at 26 volts and three-phase at 115 volts.

Much of the electrical equipment was fitted in a bay in the fuselage directly beneath the floor of the galley and forward passenger cabin.

Cabin pressurisation

The cabin pressurisation system was designed to operate at a maximum of 8¼lb/sq in at 40,000ft – about twice the pressure and twice the altitude of piston engine transports. This is a cabin pressure equivalent to 8,000ft and is essential for the well-being and comfort of passengers and crew. At lower altitudes the system was controlled to provide lower levels of cabin pressure.

BELOW The elevator control system on the Comet T2 and C2. *(www.flight-manuals-on-cd.com)*

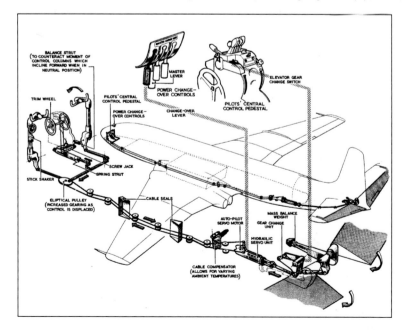

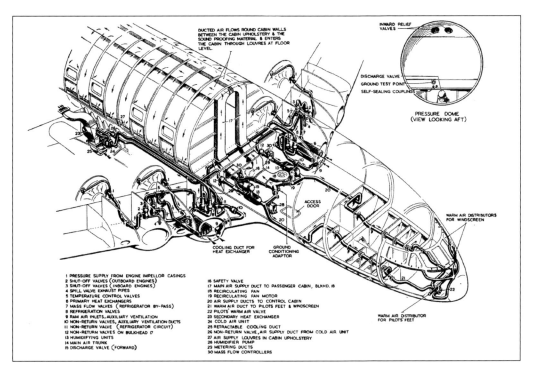

DUCTED AIR FLOWS ROUND CABIN WALLS BETWEEN THE CABIN UPHOLSTERY & THE SOUND PROOFING MATERIAL & ENTERS THE CABIN THROUGH LOUVRES AT FLOOR LEVEL.

INWARD RELIEF VALVES

DISCHARGE VALVE
GROUND TEST POINT
SELF-SEALING COUPLINGS

PRESSURE DOME
(VIEW LOOKING AFT)

ACCESS DOOR

WARM AIR DISTRIBUTORS FOR WINDSCREEN

COOLING DUCT FOR HEAT EXCHANGER

GROUND CONDITIONING ADAPTOR

WARM AIR DISTRIBUTOR FOR PILOTS' FEET

1 PRESSURE SUPPLY FROM ENGINE IMPELLOR CASINGS
2 SHUT-OFF VALVES (OUTBOARD ENGINES)
3 SHUT-OFF VALVES (INBOARD ENGINES)
4 SPILL VALVE EXHAUST PIPES
5 TEMPERATURE CONTROL VALVES
6 PRIMARY HEAT EXCHANGERS
7 MASS FLOW VALVES (REFRIGERATOR BY-PASS)
8 REFRIGERATION VALVES
9 RAM AIR INLETS, AUXILIARY VENTILATION
10 NON-RETURN VALVES, AUXILIARY VENTILATION DUCTS
11 NON-RETURN VALVE (REFRIGERATOR CIRCUIT)
12 NON-RETURN VALVES ON BULKHEAD 17
13 HUMIDIFYING UNITS
14 MAIN AIR TRUNK
15 DISCHARGE VALVE (FORWARD)
16 SAFETY VALVE
17 MAIN AIR SUPPLY DUCT TO PASSENGER CABIN, BLKHD. 18
18 RECIRCULATING FAN
19 RECIRCULATING FAN MOTOR
20 AIR SUPPLY DUCTS TO CONTROL CABIN
21 WARM AIR DUCT TO PILOTS FEET & WINDSCREEN
22 PILOTS' WARM AIR VALVE
23 SECONDARY HEAT EXCHANGER
24 COLD AIR UNIT
25 RETRACTABLE COOLING DUCT
26 NON-RETURN VALVE, AIR SUPPLY DUCT FROM COLD AIR UNIT
27 AIR SUPPLY LOUVRES IN CABIN UPHOLSTERY
28 HUMIDIFIER PUMP
29 METERING DUCTS
30 MASS FLOW CONTROLLERS

LEFT The air conditioning and pressurisation systems. (www.flight-manuals-on-cd.com)

LEFT The air conditioning and pressurisation systems. *(www.flight-manuals-on-cd.com)*

The air supply was tapped from the periphery of the compressors of each of the four Ghosts and passed through intercoolers, humidifiers and – when required – through a refrigeration unit before entering the fuselage. Apart from the refrigeration circuit, the supply from the engines in each wing was independent and either system was capable of maintaining the maximum differential pressure and correct rate of air-change. Any engine could be taken out of circuit with no loss of pressure, and each engine had an automatic control for jet-pipe temperature during cabin air delivery.

The air was at more than 200°C when bled from the compressors, flow being controlled by Saunders valves, so no separate heating system was needed and temperature control involved only the adjustment of the intercoolers and operating the refrigerator. Intercooler control was automatic, but the crew were provided with data for a manual override if necessary, while the refrigerator was switched on and off as

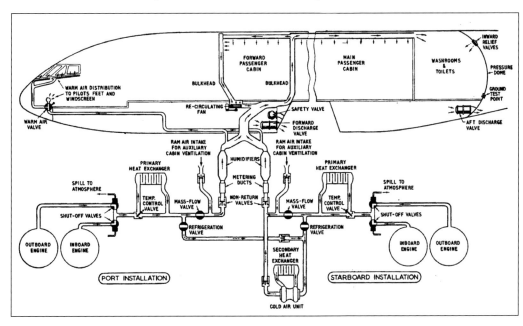

WARM AIR DISTRIBUTION TO PILOTS FEET AND WINDSCREEN

FORWARD PASSENGER CABIN

MAIN PASSENGER CABIN

WASHROOMS & TOILETS

INWARD RELIEF VALVES

PRESSURE DOME

GROUND TEST POINT

BULKHEAD

BULKHEAD

RE-CIRCULATING FAN

SAFETY VALVE

AFT DISCHARGE VALVE

WARM AIR VALVE

FORWARD DISCHARGE VALVE

RAM AIR INTAKE FOR AUXILIARY CABIN VENTILATION

HUMIDIFIERS

RAM AIR INTAKE FOR AUXILIARY CABIN VENTILATION

PRIMARY HEAT EXCHANGER

METERING DUCTS

PRIMARY HEAT EXCHANGER

SPILL TO ATMOSPHERE

TEMP. CONTROL VALVE

MASS-FLOW VALVE

NON-RETURN VALVES

MASS-FLOW VALVE

TEMP. CONTROL VALVE

SPILL TO ATMOSPHERE

SHUT-OFF VALVES

REFRIGERATION VALVE

REFRIGERATION VALVE

SHUT-OFF VALVES

OUTBOARD ENGINE

INBOARD ENGINE

INBOARD ENGINE

OUTBOARD ENGINE

PORT INSTALLATION

SECONDARY HEAT EXCHANGER

STARBOARD INSTALLATION

COLD AIR UNIT

LEFT The air conditioning system. *(www.flight-manuals-on-cd.com)*

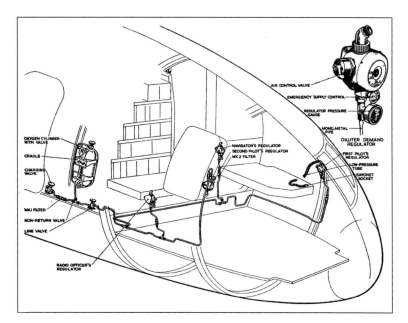

ABOVE The oxygen system of the Comet 1. *(www.flight-manuals-on-cd.com)*

in the forward under-floor bay of the fuselage, which was pressurised. Access from in the air and on the ground was quick and easy. Equipment in this bay included the humidifiers, recirculating fans, forward discharge valve and safety valve, while hydraulic equipment included the supply accumulators, cut-outs and ground-test valve.

De-icing

As with cabin pressure, the main engine compressors were tapped for delivering hot compressed air along pipes for de-icing the leading edges of the wings and tail unit. The flight deck windscreen was a double-layer dry-air sandwich, but alcohol sprays were used if necessary. The rear bearing of each Ghost was cooled by an oil flow, which was then piped round to de-ice the front of the engine, especially the front bearing. An inspection lamp was fitted to illuminate the starboard wing leading edge and air intakes to see if any ice was present.

Fuel system

Most of the fuel was contained in tanks housed in the outer wing structure, but because the wing was too thin to carry all the required tankage, a bag tank was fitted in the centre section under the cabin floor. The total weight of fuel was about 40,800lb on the Comet 1,

necessary. Each of the two circuits incorporated a humidifier, as moisture content at high altitudes is too low for comfort.

The pressure control system to limit the differential to the normal maximum was duplicated, and each part of the system could function independently. A safety valve was pre-set to operate at 8½lb/sq in.

The main components of the air-conditioning equipment were manufactured by Normalair Ltd of Yeovil in Somerset, and much of it was housed with the hydraulic and electrical systems

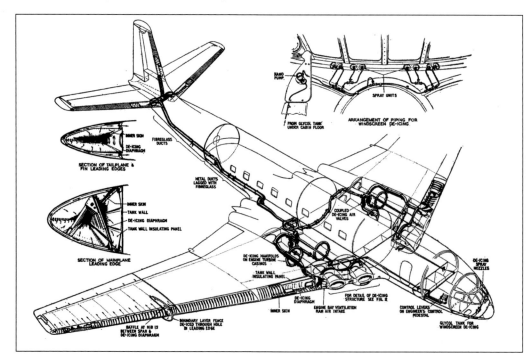

RIGHT The de-icing system on the Comet 1. *(www.flight-manuals-on-cd.com)*

but Series 1A and Series 2 had provision for an extra 1,000gal in the outer wing, bringing the maximum tankage to about 7,000gal. Feed was by two immersed booster pumps in each tank, with engine-driven pumps available in case of failure. The immersion pumps could be removed for servicing without having to drain the tanks.

The system was designed for under-wing pressure refuelling at a maximum rate of 300gal per minute, but the operation could also be carried out on top of the wing if the appropriate tankers were not available. There were two under-wing refuelling points – one on the port for the centre section and wing tanks on that side, the other on the starboard for inner and outer starboard wing tanks. The FR Mk 12 solenoid-operated filling valves were developed by Flight Refuelling Ltd of Dorset, with pressure-fuelling connections by Lockheed-Avery.

The refuelling couplings were outboard of each wheel well and, being only 6ft from the ground, were easily accessible. The valves closed automatically when a tank was filled to within 100gal of capacity. The contents of each tank could be measured from under the wing with a thin metal tube known as a dripstick. It was withdrawn downwards from the tank until fuel flowed from the open end, and thus gave a reading of the fuel level.

In-flight fuel jettisoning was actuated by ram-

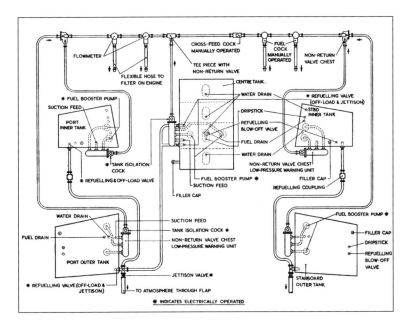

air pressure from a wing leading edge intake to drain 3,600gal from the centre section and inboard tanks on either side.

Emergency equipment

Each engine was separated into three temperature zones, which were sealed off by steel fireproof bulkheads. The individual zones had their own ventilation and fire extinguisher systems of conventional methyl-bromide and spraying type. Similar systems protected the wing leading edge equipment bay and de-icing

ABOVE Schematic of the Comet 1 fuel system. *(www.flight-manuals-on-cd.com)*

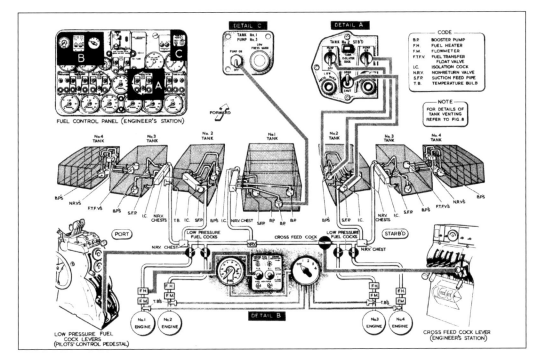

LEFT Comet T2 fuel system. *(www.flight-manuals-on-cd.com)*

RIGHT Fire protection system on the Comet T2. *(www.flight-manuals-on-cd.com)*

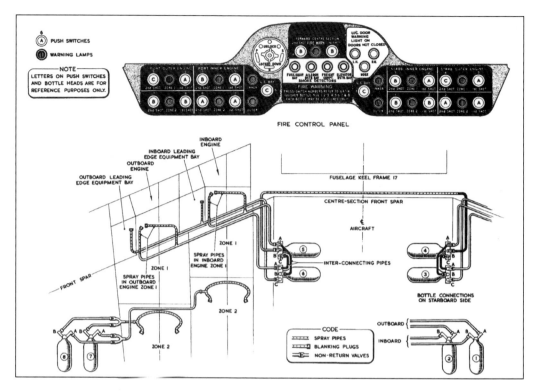

FIRE CONTROL PANEL

equipment bay and were manufactured by Graviner and Pyrene.

Fire warning lights were on the flight deck with fire extinguishing buttons on the pilots' and engineer's panels. Fire warning lights were also fitted behind each throttle lever so that trouble could be instantly identified and the relevant engine shut down. A bell sounded when either an engine fire warning or fuselage fire warning was activated.

The fuselage fire extinguishing system consisted of a semi-portable CO_2 bottle which could be plugged into sockets in the equipment bay and other under-floor zones. Portable extinguishers were also housed in the passenger cabin, flight deck and galley.

No dinghies were carried by BOAC Comets, as land was always within easy reach on the scheduled routes – but the Comet was expected to have far better flotation characteristics than most other aircraft. In the event of a belly-landing, wipe-off and inertia switches would cut off the fuel supply and electrics as well as actuating fire extinguishers and emergency lighting.

Engines

The de Havilland Ghost was a development of the Goblin engine which powered the de Havilland Vampire. It operated on the centrifugal

flow principle, whereby the incoming air was forced radially outwards to achieve compression before entering the combustion chambers.

The other type of jet engine under development at the time, notably the Rolls-Royce Avon, employed axial flow, in which the incoming air was forced into a smaller space by successive lines of compressors.

The man behind the Goblin and the Ghost was Major Frank Halford, who had a long history of designing outstanding engines, the most famous being the de Havilland Gipsy air-cooled in-line unit. In the 1920s he designed and built the Halford Special racing car in which he competed at Brooklands in the RAC British Grand Prix of 1926.

During the war he turned his attention to jet engines. His first project was the Goblin, known initially as the H-1, which was a simplified version of Whittle's centrifugal flow design. The success of this engine prompted the authorities to invite de Havilland to build a more powerful unit.

The first drawings of the Ghost were made in April 1944, when it was known as the DGT/40. It had 14 combustion chambers and an overall diameter of 57in. This was considered too big, its size being the result of the large compressor diffuser. After some redesign, cascade vanes were introduced to channel the air in a more

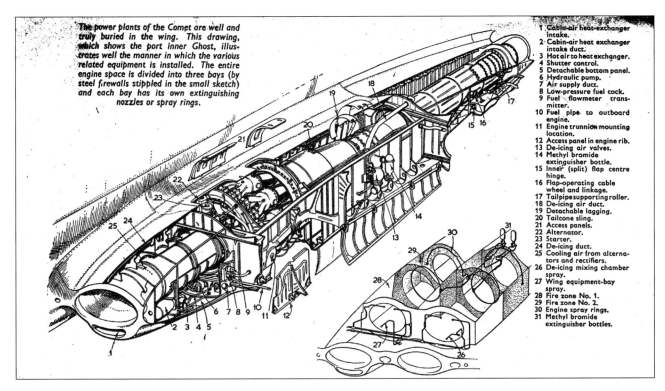

The power plants of the Comet are well and truly buried in the wing. This drawing, which shows the port inner Ghost, illustrates well the manner in which the various related equipment is installed. The entire engine space is divided into three bays (by steel firewalls stippled in the small sketch) and each bay has its own extinguishing nozzles or spray rings.

1 Cabin-air heat-exchanger intake.
2 Cabin-air heat exchanger intake duct.
3 Hot air to heat exchanger.
4 Shutter control.
5 Detachable bottom panel.
6 Hydraulic pump.
7 Air supply duct.
8 Low-pressure fuel cock.
9 Fuel flowmeter transmitter.
10 Fuel pipe to outboard engine.
11 Engine trunnion mounting location.
12 Access panel in engine rib.
13 De-icing air valves.
14 Methyl bromide extinguisher bottle.
15 Inner (split) flap centre hinge.
16 Flap-operating cable wheel and linkage.
17 Tailpipe supporting roller.
18 De-icing air duct.
19 Detachable lagging.
20 Tailcone sling.
21 Access panels.
22 Alternator.
23 Starter.
24 De-icing duct.
25 Cooling air from alternators and rectifiers.
26 De-icing mixing chamber spray.
27 Wing equipment-bay spray.
28 Fire zone No. 1.
29 Fire zone No. 2.
30 Engine spray rings.
31 Methyl bromide extinguisher bottles.

axial direction after it left the diffuser vanes. The result was an engine diameter of 53in, which was only 5in more than the Goblin.

Whereas the Goblin used 16 combustion chambers, the Ghost used 10 larger ones – but two separate outlets taken from each diffuser duct fed each chamber, giving the equivalent of 20 chambers. It was designed to be used either with a bifurcated air intake, as on the Vampire, or a direct axial intake, as on the Comet.

The redesigned engine, called the DGT/50, was first run in October 1945, and early the following year was developing its rated output of 5,000lb thrust. It was first flown in a Vampire, and later in an Avro Lancastrian, which was used to trial the engines for the Comet.

Air compressor and cooling system

The impeller was formed from a single forging in a special low-silicon heavy-duty alloy. The 19 vanes were radial throughout their length and the curved entry vanes were machined from the solid rather than bent to shape. The tubular main shaft was bolted to the rear face of the hub, while the stub shaft carrying the front main ball bearing was bolted to the front face.

The diffuser was integral with the compressor and had 20 vanes that defined the tangential

divergent ducts. Air flowing through these ducts slowed down, with a resulting increase in pressure equivalent to a compression ratio of 4.26:1 (as per Bernoulli's Principle of the relationship between pressure and speed in fluid dynamics). The air left the diffuser at a tangent before passing over four cascade vanes in each duct outlet.

A supply of cooling air was fed under pressure to an annular manifold at the rear wall of the diffuser, but during compression the temperature of this air reached 200°C, so had to be lowered to be an effective coolant. External

ABOVE Diagram showing engine installation on the Comet 1, with details of related equipment. *(Copyright unknown)*

BELOW Air-conditioning system on the Comet T2 and C2. *(www.flight-manuals-on-cd.com)*

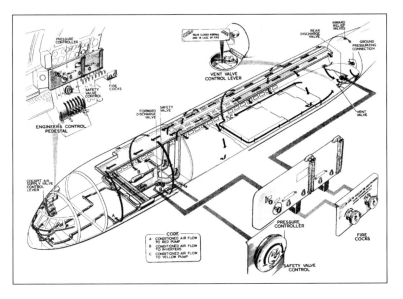

pipes conducted air from the manifold to a pair of channels in the front flange of the compressor, where it was cooled by the incoming air. A pipe from each channel delivered the air to a filter and then through an internal pipe to the rear bearing, from where it passed between the insulating plate and the front face of the turbine disc before discharging at the blades. Four external pipes from the manifold carried air to the supports of the bullet in the exhaust cone and then to the rear face of the disc.

Combustion chambers

Each combustion chamber consisted of a branched dome of light alloy, which was flanged and bolted to a mild steel outer casing. Inside the chamber was a flame tube made of Wiggins Nimonic 75 heat-resistant alloy. All chambers were interconnected to produce a pressure balance and allow the flame to spread to them when starting up.

About 30% of the air entering the dome passed the metering orifice and swirl vanes, for primary combustion of the fuel at a ratio of about 18:1. Most of it, however, flowed between the flame tube and the outer casing and was

BELOW The smooth and unrestricted intake on the prototype Comet's number two engine.

(DH4724A/BAE Systems)

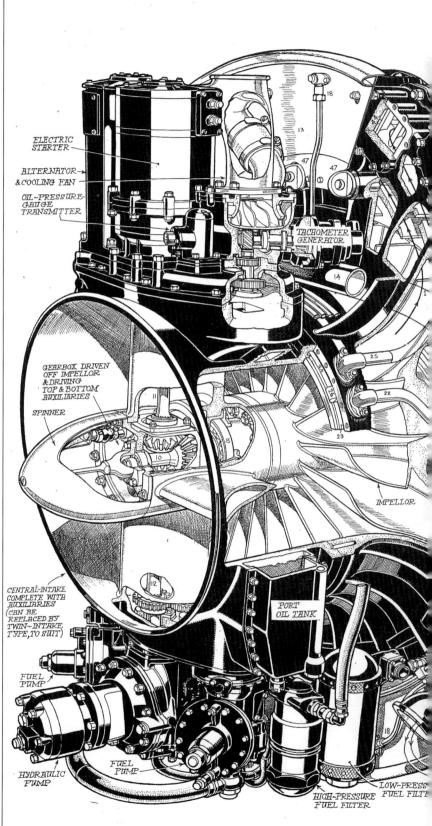

ELECTRIC STARTER

ALTERNATOR & COOLING FAN

OIL-PRESSURE-GAUGE TRANSMITTER

TACHOMETER GENERATOR

GEARBOX DRIVEN OFF IMPELLOR & DRIVING TOP & BOTTOM AUXILIARIES

SPINNER

IMPELLOR

CENTRAL-INTAKE COMPLETE WITH AUXILIARIES (CAN BE REPLACED BY TWIN-INTAKE TYPE, TO SUIT)

FUEL PUMP

FUEL PUMP

HYDRAULIC PUMP

PORT OIL TANK

HIGH-PRESSURE FUEL FILTER

LOW-PRESS FUEL FILT

The de Havilland 5,000 lb. s.t. Ghost 50 Civil Gas-turbine

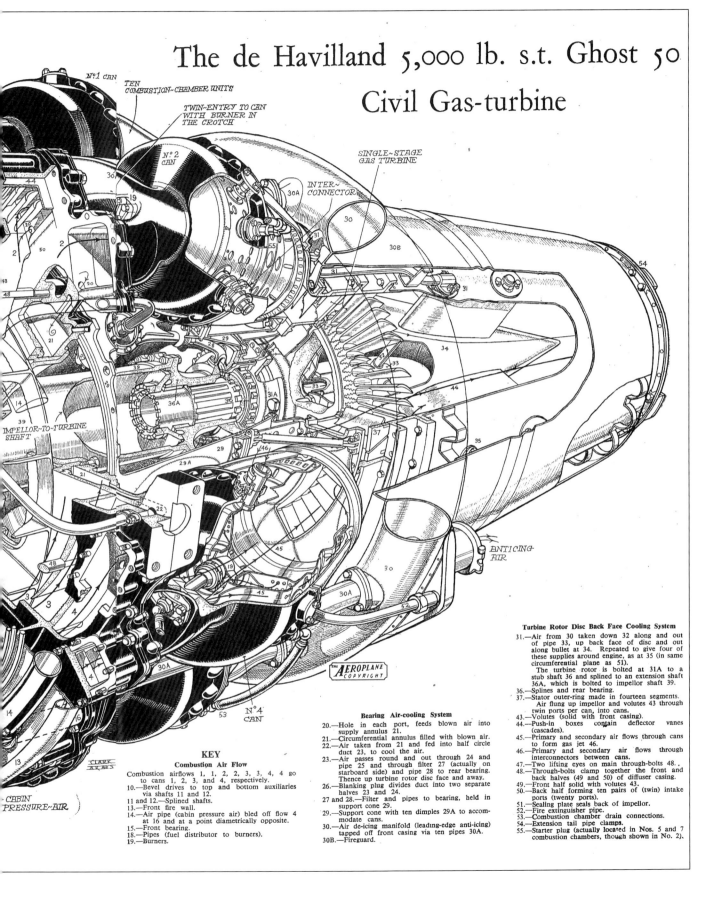

No1 CAN

TEN COMBUSTION-CHAMBER UNITS

TWIN-ENTRY TO CAN WITH BURNER IN THE CROTCH

No2 CAN

INTER-CONNECTOR

SINGLE-STAGE GAS TURBINE

IMPELLOR-TO-TURBINE SHAFT

ANTI-ICING AIR

CABIN PRESSURE-AIR

CLARK AXES

No4 CAN

THE AEROPLANE COPYRIGHT

KEY

Combustion Air Flow

Combustion airflows 1, 1, 2, 2, 3, 3, 4, 4 go to cans 1, 2, 3, and 4, respectively.
10.—Bevel drives to top and bottom auxiliaries via shafts 11 and 12.
11 and 12.—Splined shafts.
13.—Front fire wall.
14.—Air pipe (cabin pressure air) bled off flow 4 at 16 and at a point diametrically opposite.
15.—Front bearing.
18.—Pipes (fuel distributor to burners).
19.—Burners.

Bearing Air-cooling System

20.—Hole in each port, feeds blown air into supply annulus 21.
21.—Circumferential annulus filled with blown air.
22.—Air taken from 21 and fed into half circle duct 23, to cool the air.
23.—Air passes round and out through 24 and pipe 25 and through filter 27 (actually on starboard side) and pipe 28 to rear bearing. Thence up turbine rotor disc face and away.
26.—Blanking plug divides duct into two separate halves 23 and 24.
27 and 28.—Filter and pipes to bearing, held in support cone 29.
29.—Support cone with ten dimples 29A to accommodate cans.
30.—Air de-icing manifold (leading-edge anti-icing) tapped off front casing via ten pipes 30A.
30B.—Fireguard.

Turbine Rotor Disc Back Face Cooling System

31.—Air from 30 taken down 32 along and out of pipe 33, up back face of disc and out along bullet at 34. Repeated to give four of these supplies around engine, as at 35 (in same circumferential plane as 51).
The turbine rotor is bolted at 31A to a stub shaft 36 and splined to an extension shaft 36A, which is bolted to impellor shaft 39.
36.—Splines and rear bearing.
37.—Stator outer-ring made in fourteen segments. Air flung up impellor and volutes 43 through twin ports per can, into cans.
43.—Volutes (solid with front casing).
44.—Push-in boxes contain deflector vanes (cascades).
45.—Primary and secondary air flows through cans to form gas jet 46.
46.—Primary and secondary air flows through interconnectors between cans.
47.—Two lifting eyes on main through-bolts 48.
48.—Through-bolts clamp together the front and back halves (49 and 50) of diffuser casing.
49.—Front half solid with volutes 43.
50.—Back half forming ten pairs of (twin) intake ports (twenty ports).
51.—Sealing plate seals back of impellor.
52.—Fire extinguisher pipe.
53.—Combustion chamber drain connections.
54.—Extension tail pipe clamps.
55.—Starter plug (actually located in Nos. 5 and 7 combustion chambers, though shown in No. 2).

ABOVE The larger intakes of Comet 2X (G-ALYT) for the Avon 502 axial flow engines. This aircraft started life as a Comet 1 and was used for development work on the Series 2. This photo was taken on 6 June 1952, just over a month after the Series 1 went into service. *(Crown copyright)*

ABOVE RIGHT A pair of tailpipes for Comet 2X (G-ALYT) photographed in December 1951. *(DH5974A/BAE Systems)*

fed to the interior of the flame tube by a series of holes, to dilute the combustion products and lower the heat of the gas to a temperature that could be withstood by the turbine blades. A small portion of this secondary air continued to the end of the flame tube and passed through segmental slots cut in the terminal flange of the outer casing. The overall air-to-fuel ratio was about 60:1, but this would vary depending on altitude and operating conditions.

Turbine assembly

The stainless steel nozzle junction was at the discharge ends of the ten combustion chambers and was supported by a deeply dished diaphragm mounted on the housing of the rear bearing. Fixed by a flange to the rear of the nozzle junction was the 84-blade stator ring which diverted the gases to the appropriate angle of attack for the blades on the turbine wheel. Stator blades were stampings of

RIGHT An engineer makes adjustments on one of the Ghost engines in the second prototype (G-ALZK). This picture, taken in July 1950, shows how easily accessible the engines were, which made for quick turnaround times. *(DH4905B/ BAE Systems)*

Jessop's G18 B steel, and each one was secured by two integral pins riveted through the inner ring and a tongue peened in the shroud ring. To the rear of the stator ring was the shroud ring for the turbine wheel, and together these three components – nozzle junction, stator ring and turbine shroud – formed a drum.

The turbine disc was of ferrite steel instead of the more usual austenitic steel. This was favoured by de Havilland as it had sufficient mechanical strength, relatively good creep characteristics and was easier to forge.

Turbine blades

Around the periphery of the disc were 97 slots to take the 'fir tree' roots of the turbine blades, which were individual forgings in Wiggins Nimonic 80 alloy, precision machined all over to fine limits. Each blade was subjected to a virtual laboratory test, and on it was recorded the particular melt of alloy from which it was forged, its weight and moment. Blades were matched for weight and moment, and a set for a turbine wheel was built up by selective assembly.

After insertion in a segmental shroud, the disc blades were secured by peening over the fir-tree roots on both sides. The compressor impeller, main shaft and turbine wheel made up the complete rotating assembly. The large-diameter tubular shaft was machined all over and had three ribs on the circumference for balancing.

At its forward end, the shaft was bolted directly to the compressor impeller, while at the rear was a tubular extension on which the main bearing was mounted. The stub shaft of the turbine wheel entered splines in the extension and was drawn up against a large resilient washer, which clamped the inner race of the roller bearing by means of a sleeve nut located inside the main shaft.

As the rotor assembly had to operate at speeds of more than 10,000rpm it was meticulously balanced. Each of the three main components was balanced individually and then the complete assembly was dynamically balanced.

Auxiliary equipment

Auxiliary equipment was mounted on upper and lower wheel cases attached to their intake casting on the front of the compressor. The driveshaft assembly in the hub of the intake consisted of a short shaft with an integral bevel wheel, mounted on two ball bearings and driven from the end of the impeller stub shaft. The bevel wheel meshed with a pair of pinions from which the drive was taken to upper and lower wheel cases by vertical quill shafts. Distribution in the wheel cases was by spur gears.

On the upper case was the starter motor, Marshall pressurisation blower, compressor for the aircraft brakes, a 1,500W 24-volt generator for aircraft services, vacuum pump for instruments and cabin sealing, and the generator for an electric tachometer. The lower case carried the two Lucas-Ifield fuel pumps and the hydraulic pump. A spare drive was available for an additional generator on the upper wheel case.

Below the lower case was the oil sump, which had a usable capacity of 2¼gal and was cooled with air from the exhaust cone shroud. No separate oil cooler was needed. A gear-type pump provided pressure for oil drawn from the sump, and supplies were fed at specific rates to the front and rear main bearings by Tecalemit micro-metering pumps. From the front bearing the supply drained to the sump, but from the rear the surplus went to the fuel drain and was jettisoned. Maximum oil consumption was 1½pt per hour.

Fuel system

Fuel was paraffin with an added 1% of lubricating oil. From the aircraft tank the fuel was delivered by a self-priming pump through a Vokes low-pressure filter to the two Lucas-Ifield variable-stroke pumps. One pump was fitted with an overspeed device, but the servo system operated both pump controls, which were interconnected with a single barometric pressure control unit and delivered fuel past the pilot's throttle valve and the shut-off cock to a ring manifold.

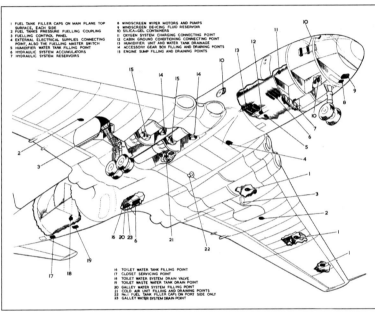

The pump circuits were linked together and controlled by a solenoid-actuated valve. If either pump failed, or if there was a problem with the piping, the pilot would be warned by a sharp drop in revs. Operation of the solenoid valve from the cockpit would automatically shut off the faulty unit and the remaining pump would take over. Fuel was delivered from the ring manifold by individual pipes to the Simplex-type burner in each combustion chamber. Closure of the shut-off cock automatically opened the dump valve and drained the fuel manifold.

TOP Rolls-Royce Avons awaiting installation on Comet 2 G-AMXA on 20 November 1953. (DH7473B/BAE Systems)

ABOVE Details of the servicing points on the Comet T2 and C2. (www.flight-manuals-on-cd.com)

Ghost specifications	
Length	121in
Diameter	53in
Dry weight	2,218lb
Combustion chambers	10
Turbine	Single stage
Fuel type	Paraffin
Maximum thrust	5,000lb at 10,250rpm

Chapter Four

Flying the Comet

The Comet took some acclimatisation for pilots used to piston engine types with their different characteristics and manually operated flying controls. The Comet's high stick break-out force and lack of feel from its servo-powered controls was disconcerting to many on the conversion course – although chief test pilot John Cunningham always seemed happy with them. But pilots soon adapted, and the prestige of being a captain on the world's first jet airliner could not be denied: they were the elite.

OPPOSITE A dramatic shot of G-ALVG against the Farnborough sky when it was demonstrated by John Cunningham at the 1949 air show. Spectators were mesmerised by its sleek lines and the whistling shriek of its Ghost engines. It seemed that the future had arrived. *(DH4298C/BAE Systems)*

ABOVE The clean and shining lines of the first prototype (G-5-1) as she is reversed out of her Hatfield hangar on 2 April 1949. There is still some work to be done on her, such as the fitting of intake nacelles, wingtips and tailcone. Part of an Avro Lancaster is visible behind her.
(Copyright unknown)

First flight

The first prototype Comet was rolled out on to the Hatfield runway in great secrecy on 25 July 1949. In gleaming natural aluminium, it looked sleek and beautiful, its only markings being the B-Conditions (British experimental) G-5-1 and the words 'DE HAVILLAND COMET' painted discreetly on the forward fuselage. But an aesthetically jarring note was struck by the incongruous and oversized single main wheel under each wing.

Over the next two days, with John Cunningham at the controls, engine runs were carried out followed by a total of 90min of taxiing and gentle hops. All was well.

The press had got wind that things were happening at Hatfield, so de Havilland's public relations officer, C. Martin Sharp, decided to invite them over to see the Comet on Wednesday 27 July. They arrived in force with cameras and notebooks, eager to get a first glimpse of what was Britain's most important new aircraft. They watched excitedly as the Comet taxied and momentarily took to the air with some short hops, then after a briefing and a spot of socialising they packed up their equipment and drove back to London. They had been led to believe it was all over for the day. It was for them – but not the Comet.

Just after they left, with the aircraft inspected and cleared for flying, Cunningham, oblivious to all other considerations, climbed back into the cockpit and at 6.17pm did just that – flew it. With him were second pilot John Wilson, flight engineer Frank Reynolds, flight test observer Tony Fairbrother and electrician Harold 'Tubby' Waters.

Sharp was in a difficult situation: if something were to go wrong on the first flight it would be a PR disaster if journalists were on the airfield. On the other hand, he knew that there would be a backlash once the press found out what they had missed.

Nothing did go wrong, and there was indeed a backlash of monumental proportions, with words such as 'arrogant' and 'unco-operative' being bandied about. The situation had not been handled well: the press felt they had been deliberately snubbed and misled, and *The Times* air correspondent vowed he would never

BELOW A view from the port side on the same day. The engine nacelles are in place on this side, and the leading edge slats can be clearly seen. These were not fitted to production aircraft, but following two serious take-off incidents, the leading edge was modified to incorporate some droop. Car enthusiasts will spot a Riley RM Series among some less exotic vehicles.
(DH4027K/BAE Systems)

RIGHT Press day at Hatfield on 27 July 1949, with the high-speed DH108 (VW120) posing alongside G-5-1. Just hours later the Comet made its first flight after the press had gone home. They were not amused at missing such a historic occasion, and made their feelings known to de Havilland's unfortunate public relations man C. Martin Sharp. (Copyright unknown)

write about de Havilland again – but the media recognised that, however hurt their feelings might have been, the Comet was too important to be ignored.

The first flight was smooth and uneventful. Before taking off, Cunningham did a short hop with full flap, holding the nose wheel off the ground until the speed had dropped to 50kt. He had the feeling he could have put the tail bumper on the runway. After taxiing back, he opened up the throttles for the first flight; and the aircraft became airborne after about 500yd, with speed increasing so rapidly that he throttled back a little.

He noticed that the ailerons appeared 'rather light, but very effective', and during the climb-out he found all the controls very powerful and highly geared, with the spring-centring producing a pronounced jerk throughout the aircraft on releasing the control column after moving it slightly.

After climbing to 10,000ft he lowered the flaps at 100kt, which resulted in very little

LEFT de Havilland's chief test pilot John Cunningham climbs aboard a Ghost-powered Vampire in March 1948 to set a world altitude record for fixed-wing aircraft of 59,492ft. (Philip J.Birtles collection)

BELOW Just hours from her historic first flight, G-5-1 at Hatfield on the afternoon of 27 July 1949. (DH6223N/BAE Systems)

ABOVE A classic shot of G-ALVG on a test flight. The BOAC Speedbird insignia is clearly visible on the nose. *(Philip J. Birtles collection)*

RIGHT John Cunningham and co-pilot John Wilson emerge from G-5-1 after her successful first flight. *(Copyright unknown)*

BELOW de Havilland personnel greet G-5-1 as she returns to the hangar after her first flight. *(Philip J. Birtles collection)*

change of trim, and even at 80kt the machine was still fully controllable. After a gradual descent, during which Cunningham found it was very hard to lose speed, he did a flypast over the Hatfield runway at 100ft for the benefit of the hundreds of clapping and cheering de Havilland personnel who had worked so hard for so long.

Landing and touchdown were uneventful after the 31min flight, and little braking was needed – partly due to a strong headwind, but it seemed to scotch comments from America (which didn't have a jet airliner) that, without the braking power of propellers, stopping distances on existing runways might be a problem. This was never an issue with the Comet.

That day heralded the start of an intense programme of flight trials and performance measurements, in which the aircraft clocked up more than an hour's flying a day for the first 110 days, sometimes putting in five flights a day. It wasn't long before the Comet was setting some impressive records, but as it was so much faster than any other civil aircraft this wasn't surprising. And considering it was such a radical departure from conventional machines, it was remarkably trouble-free, with excellent handling both on the ground and in the air.

Less than two months after its maiden flight, the Comet made its first public appearance at the Farnborough Air Show. Still in its plain aluminium finish, but now bearing the civil registration of G-ALVG, it put on a smooth and polished performance with Cunningham at the controls, the four Ghosts generating an impressive whining shriek. Things weren't quite so smooth inside the aircraft, however. Accompanying the pilot were John Wilson and

ABOVE The prototype Comet created a sensation when it was displayed at the 1949 Farnborough Air Show. Here it is captured in a quiet moment. *(Philip J. Birtles collection)*

RIGHT With its civil registration G-ALVG, the Comet sits alongside the prototype Venom (VV612) at the 1949 Farnborough Air Show. Piloted by John Derry, the Venom had made its first flight only four days before the show opened on 6 September. *(DH4297K/BAE Systems)*

Chris Beaumont, chief test pilot of the de Havilland Engine Company. Wilson later recalled that each time Cunningham banked and pulled 2½–3g the floor under Beaumont's feet bulged up, and during the low flypast at 340kt – very fast for a new aircraft – there was a loud bang, which was from the fuselage skin.

But the test programme proceeded well, and on 8 August the Comet had touched Mach 0.8 in a shallow dive; then in November it reached an altitude of 43,000ft on a flight in which it went from Edinburgh to Brighton in 42min – an average speed of 530mph. A few days later G-ALVG covered the 590 miles from the Shetland Islands to Hatfield in 60min, during a flight at operational height that lasted more than five hours.

With a cruising speed at 40,000ft of 490mph, city-to-city records began to tumble with ease, and the test programme took the

RIGHT An atmospheric study of G-ALVG as she flies past the Farnborough crowds in September 1949 towards the famous Black Sheds. *(DH4298B/BAE Systems)*

Comet to more hostile climatic locations such as Nairobi, where tropical trials were carried out, and to Khartoum where temperatures were very high at low altitudes.

In October 1949, G-ALVG flew to Castel Benito airport in Tripoli in 3hr 23min, an average speed of 434mph, much of which was spent cruising at 500mph. This convincingly swept aside all that had gone before, as the same trip in the fastest Lockheed Constellation would take 5hr.

The second prototype (G-ALZK), which took to the air exactly a year after the first, was delivered to BOAC on 2 April 1951. Over the next six months it made 12 overseas tours for route-proving and to gain practical experience in the new operating techniques at various locations.

BELOW Comet 1 pre-flight check list. (www.flight-manuals-on-cd.com)

Pilot training

A major undertaking before the aircraft could enter service was the implementation of a thorough training programme for pilots and service personnel. The de Havilland Service School had for many years offered comprehensive courses for customers' aircrews and maintenance engineers, but conversion to the Comet, with its jet engines and new operating systems, called for something much more specialised.

Elaborate demonstration rigs to simulate the Comet and its systems were installed in an old hangar at Hatfield. These included a cockpit mock-up where the pilot could operate the flying controls and undercarriage, and also handle the kind of emergencies and faults that might be experienced in flight, all of which were generated artificially and, of course, without a computer. Students were able to see and become familiar with all aspects of the Comet with the aid of individual rigs to demonstrate the fuel system, power control operation, hydraulics bay and even a complete undercarriage that retracted and lowered.

People do not always take kindly to change,

PRE-FLIGHT ACTION AND INSPECTION
(Note: throughout these notes the abbreviation P/E stands for 2nd Pilot or Engineer.)

(Action by: all crew)
- Check loading instructions for fuel and fuel usage, centres of gravity (C of G) to be experienced, passenger and ballast (if any) disposition and freight loading.
- *Note:* it is important that NO fire extinguishers containing carbon-tetrachloride shall be carried in the cabins.

EXTERNAL INSPECTION
(Action by: P/E)
- Check that the aircraft is in a suitable position for starting having due regard for the temperature and force of the jet efflux.
- Check wheels chocked.
- Check air intake and tail pipe covers removed.
- Check pitot head covers removed.
- Check all inspection covers under wing for security.
- Check fuel blow off handles for locking.

Main undercarriage
- Check undercarriage wheel well, ascertaining that no tools, etc. have been left behind, and check door for security.
- Check hydraulic connections for leaks.
- Check general condition, etc. of electric cables.
- Check ground locking pins removed.
- Inspect hose brake lines for evidence of wear and hydraulic leaks.
- Check wheel tyres for condition and tyre creep.
- Check refuelling panel doors locked.

Nose undercarriage
- Generally as for main undercarriage.

General
- Check flap and control surface, disposition and aircraft skin generally for wrinkles, cracks, and fuel or oil leaks.
- Check that all hatches are closed and *fully* locked, i.e. that the hatch handles have been turned to the full extent of their travel.
- Ground power plugged in and ready for starting.

ON ENTERING AIRCRAFT
(Action by: P/E)
Commencing from rear of aircraft
- Check passenger entry door for security and handle for locking.

- Check (under floor) rudder and elevator servo units for general disposition and evidence of hydraulic leaks in the drip trays provided.
- Check that dust cover has been removed from rear discharge valve.
- Check all cabin escape hatch levers for security.
- Check all silica gel containers for content and crystal colour.
- Look through cabin windows and check that all wing top surface and engine inspection panels are secure.
- Check thoroughly cabin windows for crazing.
- Check all seats for security and provision of safety harness.

Rear luggage bay
- Check disposition of freight (if any) with Load Sheet.
- Check disposition, generally, of aileron servo unit and yellow pump system, and look for evidence of hydraulic leaks in drip trays provided.
- Check pressure of yellow system accumulator.
- Check pressure of undercarriage door accumulators.

Equipment bay
- Generally check whole bay for hydraulic and water leaks, cable and pipe runs for fouling and deterioration.
- Check that humidifier tanks are full.
- Check hydraulic reservoirs for content.
- Check hydraulic accumulators for pressure.
- Check that the four alternator circuit breakers are set.
- Check that the starter circuit breaker is set.
- Check 'Ground test' handle for security and position.
- Check that dust covers have been removed from discharge and safety valves.
- Check that handpump is stowed correctly.
- Set all requisite circuit breakers for flight, leaving 'Acc. Relay' off until power is actually required.
- Put cockpit instrument switches ON and check fuel tank contents with Load Sheet.
- Check that 'Undercarriage Emergency' lever is OFF.
- Check that 'Fuel transfer' lever is OFF.
- Check that 'De-icing' levers are OFF.
- Check silica-gel containers for content and crystal colour.
- Generally check the whole of the flight deck ensuring that all switches and cocks are OFF, that seat guides are free of dirt and easy to operate and that oxygen supply is full; see that oxygen is turned fully on at the bottle and check pressure at each regulator.
- Check that CL2 compass switch is selected for PILOT.

and there were heated discussions among some pilots on the conversion course. Military pilots were familiar with power controls, bogie undercarriages and air brakes, but to the airline pilot all this was new. There were those who couldn't understand why equipment that had served them well for many years was not being used on the Comet, but at the end of the course they understood the need for these changes and could see that a huge amount of thought had gone into developing first-class ancillaries for the aircraft.

The seven-week course was split into periods studying the Ghost 50 engine, the airframe and its hydraulic systems, electrics, pressurisation, emergency procedures, aircraft flying limitations, loading and instrumentation. Several visits were also made to the Comet production line.

Before actual flying experience there was an ARB examination consisting of about 100 questions in order to gain a licence endorsement for a pilot or engineer to operate as a crew member on passenger-carrying services. This was followed by flying experience.

In the air

Climbing aboard through the crew entrance on the starboard side of the nose, the aircrew had to duck a little to enter beneath the sliding door. The engineer carried out a comprehensive external checklist, checking fuel contents by the dripsticks, inspecting all surfaces, wheels, cowlings, brake leads, and removing the three ground locking pins in the undercarriage. He would then make an internal check of emergency exits, safety equipment,

the baggage bay beneath the cabin floor and the equipment bay. These two bays were accessible in flight, as were the Servodynes which actuated the flying controls.

On the flight deck, the captain began the 'before starting engines' check from a list read by the first officer. Flying controls were verified on the yellow (emergency) hydraulic system, and cockpit controls were set for starting. The Smiths SEP 1 autopilot was checked in all three axes and the 'limit cut-out' switches tested to ensure disengagement if any of the flying control surfaces were moved outside the narrow limits (this autopilot safeguard ensured that faulty operation couldn't put the aircraft in a dangerous attitude).

The first officer checked that all warning lights were working, as well as the hooter which warned of hydraulic pressure loss in the main flying-control system, the engine-fire warning bells and the smoke detectors in the fuselage bays. Tank-isolator cocks were selected to 'on' for all wing tanks and the cross-feed was checked 'off'. The first officer would then contact air traffic control (ATC) and request clearance to start up. This was a change from normal piston engine practice and was owing to the very high fuel consumption of jet engines idling on the ground, which was about 8gal a minute. Time spent with thirsty engines idling was money lost.

After clearance it was the 'starting engines check': throttles were closed, isolation switches set to 'normal', the ground engineer was alerted, and with the starter master-switch 'on' and low- and high-pressure cocks 'on', the start sequence was initiated. Either number one or number four engine was started first. With the selector set for

ABOVE Still with the single main gear wheel, G-ALVG undergoing proving trials for BOAC. A Saunders-Roe Skeeter helicopter can be seen on the far left of the picture. *(N.D. Welch)*

79

FLYING THE COMET

ABOVE Now sporting the four-wheel bogie main gear that would be used on all production Comets, G-ALVG makes an elegant sight in the Hatfield sunshine. *(DH4496B/BAE Systems)*

BELOW G-ALVG touches down at Hatfield during trials of the new undercarriage. The huge flaps are well displayed in this picture. *(DH4496A/BAE Systems)*

the appropriate engine, the single starter button was depressed to operate the 30-second starting cycle. The button was held in by an electrical relay until the cycle was complete.

With all four engines idling at 3,000rpm, the starting procedure was completed by checking flying-control operation on the blue (normal) hydraulic system. Alternators were checked for correct operation, voltage and load-sharing, engine instruments for correct temperatures and pressures, and then a final confirmation that AC failure lights and door warning lights were out, followed by the Zero Reader check and alignment of the CL2 compass. Radio equipment, including the twin auto direction-finders and the ILS and marker receivers, were tested and tuned for take-off procedures.

With chocks away and parking brake off, the outboard engines were opened up to about 6,000rpm, the inners remaining at 3,000rpm to save fuel. When the aircraft began to move, the outers were throttled to about 4,500rpm to keep a moderately high taxi speed.

While taxiing to the take-off position, the 'before take-off' check was completed. Flying instruments were examined for serviceability, and the blue pressure-failure warning horn was switched on. Flying controls were checked finally on the blue system, flaps were set to 15° and aileron, elevator and rudder trims at take-off setting, air brakes 'off' and pitot heaters on. Critical speed (V1) and unstick speed (V2) were then read out.

When all instruments had been checked, the engine fuel pump isolation solenoids were switched to 'isolate' and back to 'normal'.

LEFT Although Comet testing was dominating de Havilland's programme, flight trials of the slow-speed DH108 (TG283) continued. The other two had been lost in high-speed crashes, and on 1 May 1950 TG283 joined them when young Farnborough test pilot Eric 'Jumbo' Genders was unable to recover from a flat spin. He died next to the wreckage at Hartley Wintney in Hampshire, unable to get clear of the aircraft in time to open his parachute. Three aircraft lost, three lives lost – no wonder famous test pilot Eric 'Winkle' Brown called it a serial killer, and no wonder the format was unsuitable for an airliner. *(Copyright unknown)*

Pressurisation controls, fuel tank booster pumps, fuel feed, thermal de-icing, emergency hydraulic selector, alternator, instrument (26V) and main (115V) inverters, fuel flow meter, fuel contents gauges and cabin air conditioning would have been set correctly by the engineer as called out from the checklist by the first officer.

Throttles were opened slowly until the jet-pipe temperature reached 500°C and then the levers were moved progressively forward (recommended time from idling to full opening was 10sec). With the four Ghosts running at 10,200rpm, the isolation controls were switched to 'isolate' and engine revs rose to 10,250rpm. The first officer and engineer would make a final inspection of all engine instruments, and then the parking brake was released. At this point fuel consumption was at its highest, and delays had to be kept to a minimum.

The Comet accelerated quickly, giving the crew a kick in the back almost from the beginning of the take-off run. Nose-wheel steering was used up to around 60kt when the rudder became effective and, in accordance with the BOAC Comet manual, at 80kt the nose was raised until the rumble of the wheel ceased, but the pilot had to be careful not to adopt an exaggerated tail-down attitude with consequent poor acceleration. Once in the air the Comet accelerated rapidly and continuously. The undercarriage was raised by the first officer, which resulted in a slight nose-up change of trim, and speed allowed to increase to 150kt with a flap setting of 15° to give the optimum angle of climb. Fuel pump isolation switches were moved to 'normal' at 100ft and engine revs reduced to 9,750.

Flaps were raised at between 500 and 1,000ft and speed built up to the correct cruising-climb figure of 260kt indicated airspeed. The pilot's feet were removed from the rudder pedals and not replaced until the approach. This was to avoid over-stressing the rudder at high speeds and to give greater passenger comfort. Turns were made on ailerons alone.

Unlike piston engine airliners, the Comet would accelerate very quickly if the nose was lowered a few degrees, and it would be all too easy at cruise height to exceed the limiting Mach number of 0.77, or an IAS (indicated

airspeed) of 300kt. The airspeed indicator did not respond quickly enough to show any change in pitch, so the most reliable instrument was the vertical speed indicator.

New pilots found the lack of feel to the controls very disconcerting at first, as there was no indication of the loads being applied: the stick force for aileron operation remained constant, regardless of whether the aircraft was on the ground or flying at high speed. The only resistance was in overcoming the initial 40lb spring strut which biased each set of cables on the Servodyne inputs. If the pilot let go of the column after moving it away from the trimmed point, it would snap back to that position very smartly. The only way was to guide the column firmly and steadily back to the trimmed position.

Cabin pressurisation was controlled by the engineer, who maintained the flow of air tapped from the engine compressors at a constant level to avoid surges. He also had to keep an eye out for any automatic equipment problem, checking

ABOVE The second Comet prototype (G-ALZK) undergoes engine runs at Hatfield on 27 July 1950, a few hours before its first flight – a year to the day after the first prototype's maiden flight. *(BAE Systems)*

BELOW Seconds after leaving the runway, G-ALZK is captured on camera just as the undercarriage is retracting. *(DH4932L/ BAE Systems)*

ABOVE **A beautiful study of the two prototype Comets, G-ALVG in BOAC livery and G-ALZK, as they fly over the countryside on 4 September 1950.** *(DH4973B/BAE Systems)*

BELOW **A charming picture taken on 23 June 1951 of Sir Geoffrey de Havilland with Princess Margaret on the Comet flight deck. In the first officer's seat is John Cunningham.** *(DH5617A/BAE Systems)*

the cabin differential pressure up to a maximum of 8¼lb/sq in. Any change in engine revs called for rapid adjustment of the mass-flow valves, with which the automatic equipment did not always cope. The engineer also had to record and integrate fuel-flow readings to give a constant check of weight and fuel on board.

If the Comet went beyond its normal never-exceed indicated Mach number of 0.77, there would be a mild nose-down change of trim, and if this was not corrected a dangerous situation could develop with the speed rising indefinitely. All crews had to do a training flight in which the aircraft was taken to Mach 0.81 indicated at around 40,000ft so that they knew what to expect, and how to correct it with nothing more than slight up-elevator.

Stalling

Stalling was, of course, not something that would normally be encountered during passenger service, but it was an important part of aircrew training, as were other emergency procedures. With undercarriage and flaps up and throttles closed, the nose would be held up to decrease airspeed until a severe pre-stall buffeting set in. But, once again, the irreversible power controls with their lack of feel transmitted no information to the pilot's hands that a stall was approaching – although the shaking airframe gave its own unmistakable message.

The warning signs began at 10kt before the stall at indicated speeds of 98kt and 115kt at weights of 75,000lb and 105,000lb respectively. With wheels down and 15° of flap, similar buffeting happened before the stall. With flap-settings of 40° or 60°, and power on or off, the warning was less severe and either wing could be picked up before it dropped more than 20°. Stalling speeds at 75,000lb with full flap were about 90kt (power on) and 96kt (power off), but with power on, the nose dropped suddenly.

Pilots considered the stalling characteristics benign, and even with the Ghosts on one side throttled back and the other two at 9,750rpm, the rudder had strong authority right up to the point of stall. Height lost was rarely more than 500ft.

Landing

Handling the Comet at low levels around an airfield was not so different from piston engine aircraft, and speeds were nothing out of the ordinary: downwind, 150kt with 15° flap; crosswind, 135kt with wheels down and 40° flap; final turn, 125kt. The approach path was held with engines at 7,000–8,000rpm and adjustments of 500rpm to keep the aircraft on the correct glide path. Full flap of 60° altered the flight path considerably with a nose-up change of trim, and the usual practice was to select this earlier than normal to compensate for the lag in rpm response on the approach and the change in flight path, so the pilot needed good judgement and anticipation – more so than on piston engine machines.

Final stages of the approach were at 110–115kt, and the runway threshold was crossed at 100–105kt. But, again owing to the lack of control feel, and also the short nose, the aircraft's attitude could be hard to judge. Brakes were applied steadily as soon as the nose wheel was on the ground, and the elevator trim was wound fully forward to give maximum traction. An after-landing check completed the flight.

Emergencies

Pilots received comprehensive theoretical and practical training in emergency procedures. With a training captain beside him, the pilot would perform a series of basic instrument manoeuvres, including 'recovery from unusual positions', such as a spiral dive or sustained high-G turn. Engine re-lighting and fire drills were also carried out, followed by a homing to a radio aid on basic instruments.

After obtaining clearance inbound, the pilot made his approach and landing on full instruments, normally using ILS and with one

LEFT Taken in September 1951, this picture shows the prototype de Havilland DH110 (WG236) at Hatfield with the second production Comet (G-ALYR). WG236 first flew on the 26th of that month piloted by John Cunningham, but judging by the tape over the observer's hatch and lack of ejection seat warning triangle, this picture was almost certainly taken before that. The following year WG236 went supersonic many times at the hands of John Derry, accompanied by flight test observer Tony Richards. (DH5745D/BAE Systems)

RIGHT The beauty of the Comet is evident in this picture of the second prototype (G-ALZK) in BOAC livery. *(BAE Systems)*

BELOW Certificate of Airworthiness for G-ALYS, the first Comet to be delivered to BOAC. *(DH6046/BAE Systems)*

M.C.A. Form No. 958

UNITED KINGDOM

MINISTRY OF CIVIL AVIATION

CERTIFICATE OF AIRWORTHINESS

No. A.3215

NATIONALITY AND REGISTRATION MARKS	CONSTRUCTOR AND CONSTRUCTOR'S DESIGNATION OF AIRCRAFT	AIRCRAFT SERIAL No. (CONSTRUCTOR'S No.)
G-ALYS	The de Havilland Aircraft Co. Ltd. Comet D.H.106 Series 1.	06005
CATEGORY :	Normal	
SUBDIVISION :	(a) Public transport for passengers (b) Public transport for mails (c) Public transport for goods (d) Private (e) Aerial work (h) Demonstration (i) Crew familiarisation	

This Certificate of Airworthiness is issued pursuant to the Convention on International Civil Aviation dated 7th December, 1944, and the Air Navigation Order, 1949, the Air Navigation (General) Regulations, 1949, and the Air Navigation (Radio) Regulations, 1949, in respect of the above-mentioned aircraft, which is considered to be airworthy when maintained and operated in accordance with the requirements of the above-mentioned Order and Regulations, and the pertinent Flight Manual.

John S. mulley.
~~Director General~~ Minister of Civil Aviation.

Date 22nd January, 1952.

This certificate is valid for the period(s) shewn below

Signature, Official Stamp and Date

From 22nd January, 1952.	to 21st January, 1953.	
From	to	
From	to	
From	to	
From	to	

No entries or endorsements may be made on this Certificate except in the manner and by the persons authorised for the purpose by the Minister of Civil Aviation.

If this Certificate is lost, the Secretary, Ministry of Civil Aviation (R.L.2) should be informed at once, the Certificate Number being quoted.

Any person finding this Certificate should forward it immediately to the Secretary, Ministry of Civil Aviation. (R.L.2), Ariel House, Strand, London, W.C.2.

(9154) Wt. 9796 J938 900 4 49 C.& Co. 745(8)

or two engines inoperative. Finally, various instructors would sign out the pilot, who could then apply to the Ministry of Civil Aviation for a Comet endorsement to his licence at a fee of two guineas (£2.10).

The final stage in Comet conversion training was route familiarisation. A captain would complete two full trips on any particular route before being authorised to operate in command, while first officers and navigators were also given two full supervised trips. After that, he was a fully fledged Comet captain.

The passenger's view

One man lucky enough to get a flight in the Comet a few months before the first scheduled passenger service was C.B. Bailey-Watson, technical editor of *Flight* magazine. He and some French VIPs went aboard the first production Comet (G-ALYP) and were taken on a 1,000-mile tour over France with John Cunningham at the helm.

'I experienced a degree of enjoyment which comes my way but rarely,' he wrote, 'so much so that it is not easy to keep enthusiasm within the bounds of the accuracy which factual description demands.'

Bailey-Watson was sitting in the eight-seat compartment ahead of the main cabin and was facing towards the rear. As they taxied out to the Hatfield runway they watched John Derry take off in the prototype DH110 (WG236), an event which caused a ripple of excitement for the French guests.

Moments later the Comet was airborne. 'The acceleration seemed to be less marked than one experiences in airscrew-driven airliners, and the initial climbing angle was scarcely perceptible in terms of seat attitude. What was so very impressive was the tremendous sense of height gained and forward speed: one expects it in a fighter,

ABOVE A dramatic shot of the third production Comet, G-ALYS, but not quite convincing enough to be real. *(DH6088/BAE Systems)*

BELOW A rare shot of the prototype Comet (G-ALVG) in BOAC colours and sporting the pinion fuel tanks that would feature on the Comet 3 and 4. The date is unknown, but she still has the single-wheel main gear, which is almost obscured by the de Havilland personnel posing with her. *(DH7201/BAE Systems)*

ABOVE The first prototype (G-ALVG) displaying at the 1950 Farnborough Air Show.
(BAE Systems)

RIGHT Above the clouds in brilliant sunshine on 28 March 1951. In the foreground is G-ALYP, the Comet which would make the world's first commercial jetliner flight. With her are the two prototypes G-ALVG and G-ALZK.
(DH5402H/BAE Systems)

RIGHT Air France ordered three Comet 1As. This one, F-BGNY, is pictured on 20 May 1953. *(DH7040B/BAE Systems)*

but not when one is seated in a comfortable armchair.'

He found it was 'astonishingly quiet' in the forward cabin – even quieter than he had expected. 'Livid masses of cloud flew past, and quick ripples of cobblestone-bumping made the aircraft quiver, whilst the wing tip seemingly almost lazily flexed to the turbulence: and then we were in the glittering effulgence of clear sunlight, brilliantly reflected from the snowfield of stratocumulus below.'

Bailey-Watson had a wander through the main cabin, sitting in different seats to check noise and vibration levels. The least quiet spot was the front row of the main cabin, where the seats were nearest to the engine compressors – but he liked the noise: 'A medium-pitched hum which I can best liken to that wonderful sound one hears from an Alfa cruising at 80mph.'

Further aft, things became progressively quieter – but he stressed that even the loudest point in the cabin was considerably quieter than on piston engine aircraft. This, combined with the lack of vibration, put the Comet in a league of its own for passenger comfort. 'I have never flown so quietly or so smoothly in anything,' he remarked. And he concluded: 'One knows that the Comet will put existing airliners in the shade; but truly one has to fly in it to realise how wholly dissatisfied passengers will be with other types once they have experienced Comet travel.'

Summary

Pilots and passengers alike were enthusiastic about the Comet, but it was inevitable that a jet airliner was going to entail operating and flying techniques that were different from propeller-driven aircraft.

The lack of noise and vibration was welcomed by everyone, as were the speed and flight characteristics. But pilots did not generally enjoy the lack of feel to the controls, which could be likened to driving a car with very light power steering that did not transmit any information to the driver from the front wheels.

ABOVE One of the two Comet 1A transports for the Royal Canadian Air Force. *(BAE Systems)*

BELOW The Comet 2X (G-ALYT) on her maiden flight on 16 February 1952. She was a Comet 1 fitted with Avon engines for development trials of the Comet 2. *(Philip J. Birtles collection)*

Chapter Five

The Comet in service

The day the Comet took off on its first scheduled passenger flight was a historic occasion that marked the start of air travel as we know it today. For months the Comet reigned supreme, making all that came before it seem almost obsolete, as though from another era. In the brave new Elizabethan age of exploration, Britain ruled the skies. Not until Concorde would there be anything like this.

OPPOSITE Passengers alight from G-ALYS, the third production Comet, at Johannesburg. It was an era of optimism, elegance and excitement as air travel entered a new age. *(DHT673CP/BAE Systems)*

RIGHT An evocative and artistic advertisement by Lockheed for their Servodyne power control system and hydraulics on the Comet. This image encapsulates the optimism and excitement of jet passenger travel.

LOCKHEED HYDRAULICS ON THE 'COMET'

For the controls on an air liner of such high performance as the de Havilland 'Comet,' accurate and responsive Servo assistance is essential.

For that reason the Lockheed 'Servodyne' system has been employed since the inception of this fine aircraft; it is powered by the Lockheed engine-driven pump. The complete Lockheed system of hydraulics is also used.

*REGD. TRADE MARK.

ALL-BRITISH Lockheed
AUTOMOTIVE PRODUCTS COMPANY LTD., Leamington Spa.

Experience

BOAC set up a special Comet Unit in September 1950 to prepare for passenger service and, while awaiting delivery of the second prototype for trials, the unit concentrated on route analyses and engineering aspects, as well as getting flying experience with the Hatfield test team. Meanwhile, the Ministry of Civil Aviation had been holding 'Jet Operations Working Party' meetings to finalise the many requirements of jet airliner service and to study the Comet's performance in relation to the ATC system then being developed.

When the Comet Unit received G-ALZK on 2 April 1951 they were well briefed on what was needed to integrate the aircraft on regular passenger schedules. Intense performance and route-proving trials were carried out, including holding and descent procedures, where it was found that the Comet fitted in with normal ATC patterns, even at busy airports in bad weather conditions, and could happily mix with piston engine airliners.

Everything was leading up to the momentous day when the Comet would inaugurate the world's first jet airliner service. That day was to be Friday 2 May 1952, but in the meantime Prince Philip was taken for a flight in G-ALYP on 13 March, spending much of the time on the flight deck.

By the end of April the corporation had four Comet 1s in its fleet. G-ALYS was delivered on 31 December 1951, followed over the next few months by G-ALYU, G-ALYP and G-ALYV. Its third aircraft, G-ALYP, known as Yoke Peter in the phonetic alphabet of the time, the one in which Bailey-Watson had his memorable trip, was selected for the historic occasion, operating as flight BA113 out of London Airport, destination Johannesburg.

BELOW G-ALYP at Hatfield. She was selected by BOAC for the world's first commercial flight of a jet airliner.
(Copyright unknown)

A throng of spectators and media representatives had arrived to watch the take-off, including Sir Geoffrey de Havilland along with board members of de Havilland and BOAC. Once the last of the 36 passengers had boarded, little time was wasted, and 3min after the door was closed the engine start-up procedure was initiated. Moments later, at 3pm, G-ALYP taxied out to the runway, looking graceful and refined in the corporation's understated fuselage decor of gloss white upper surface, royal blue cheat strip along the plane of the windows, with two further strips on the fin and the rest of the airframe in natural aluminium.

With a crew of six, headed by Captain Michael Majendie at the controls, 36

LEFT The BOAC airport bus about to take passengers out to Comet G-ALYP for the first fare-paying flight in a jet airliner. *(DH9124/BAE Systems)*

RIGHT A moment these passengers would never forget as they board G-ALYP at London Airport on 2 May 1952. *(DH6291A/BAE Systems)*

BELOW The de Havilland photographer captures Charles Sims capturing a historic occasion for *The Aeroplane* as the first fare-paying passengers board G-ALYP on 2 May 1952. *(DH6283Y/BAE Syste*

BELOW RIGHT BOAC personnel wave G-ALYP off on the afternoon of 2 May 1952 as she taxies out to the London Airport runway to make the world's first commercial flight of a jet airliner. *(British Airways)*

ABOVE She's off! A historic moment is captured on camera as G-ALYP lifts off from London Airport on her flight to Johannesburg on 2 May 1952. *(Copyright unknown)*

BELOW This is what it was like inside: travellers relax in the comfortable seats of the Comet on a flight in 1952. *(DH7443V/BAE Systems)*

passengers and 30 bags of mail, the Comet was airborne at 3.12pm, bound for Rome, the first of five stops on the 6,724-mile journey to South Africa. It arrived at Johannesburg 23hr 37min later, just 3min ahead of schedule. That was the day that air travel changed for ever. Airlines throughout the world knew well in advance that they had a simple choice: order Comets or be left behind.

The initial batch of ten Comets was followed by ten of the improved 1A version, which had its fuel capacity increased by 1,000gal to 6,909gal and gross weight up from 105,000lb to 115,000lb. The extra fuel, which was in the wings, gave a 20% increase in operating range. Water-methanol injection was also available, giving 10–12% more thrust at take-off, which was the equivalent of lowering the ambient temperature by about 10°C.

An early order for two 1As was placed by Canadian Pacific in December 1949, with a further two for the Royal Canadian Air Force (RCAF), and it was the RCAF ones which became the first jet airliners to cross the Atlantic when they were delivered in June 1953, as well as the first jet transports to enter military service. Three 1As were ordered by UAT (Union Aeromaritime de Transport) in May 1951 and a further three by Air France in November the same year.

Although the focus was on BOAC for having inaugurated jet travel, the private French airline UAT, which was the second in the world to

RIGHT The giant catering company J. Lyons and Co. Ltd had been experimenting for two years with frozen cooked food, and it was served with great success on airlines as 'Frood'. GEC designed a special oven for heating these dishes in the aircraft galley, and every item was cooked, frozen and heated separately so that passengers could make individual choices, as opposed to the American 'pre-dished' frozen meals. Almost every kind of food was suitable for the process, and it could be stored for more than a year without deteriorating. *(Copyright unknown)*

Frood on the Comet — means heavenly eating!

Frood travels B·O·A·C and other leading airlines

FROOD IS MADE BY J. LYONS & CO. LTD., CADBY HALL, LONDON. W.14

operate the Comet, was extremely proud of its three Comet 1As, which entered passenger service in February 1953 with a seven-times-a-week service between Paris or Marseilles to French Africa. Purchasing the Comet was a big step for a small airline, but their enthusiasm and thoroughness won the day, and by April they had extended their routes to Brazzaville, the capital of French Equatorial Africa, achieving excellent punctuality. This was thanks to highly efficient maintenance at their base and detailed planning for their operations.

Air France took delivery of their first aircraft in June, which entered service in August on their Beirut schedule, followed by Algiers and Cairo.

BELOW LEFT *The Aeroplane* published a beautifully produced special edition on 2 May 1952 to mark the first commercial flight of the Comet. Packed with in-depth articles, many illustrations and artistic advertisements, it was a fitting memento of the occasion. *(Aeroplane)*

BELOW Personal service, decent food, comfort, smoothness – that was Comet travel in the early 1950s. This picture was taken aboard BOAC's Comet G-ALYS. *(DH5783A/BAE Systems)*

THE AEROPLANE
MAY 2, 1952
EVERY FRIDAY ONE SHILLING

Great Britain introduces the world's first jet airliner
DE HAVILLAND
DE HAVILLAND COMET AIRCRAFT WITH DE HAVILLAND GHOST JET ENGINES

RIGHT AND BELOW
**Colourful BOAC
advertisements for
Comet travel in the
early 1950s.**
(British Airways)

Everyone wanted to fly on the Comet, and passengers marvelled at the smoothness and the wonder of being able to see the world from altitudes they had never experienced, well above the turbulent weather that was so often the lot of conventional aircraft. On 30 June 1953 the Queen Mother and Princess Margaret were guests on a special four-hour flight in G-ALYR hosted by Sir Geoffrey and Lady de Havilland, which took in France, Switzerland and northern Italy, before returning home across the Pyrenees.

The superiority of the Comet over piston engine airliners was brought into sharp focus in August 1953, when BOAC launched a nine-stop London to Tokyo service by Comet which took 36 hours. The same journey in an Argonaut took 86hr 35min. The corporation did not open the Tokyo service until it had carried out nine months of thorough route-proving and familiarisation experience for many captains and crews.

By the end of the first year of operation, BOAC Comets had clocked up 9,443 flying hours and carried 28,000 passengers, with 61% of all arrivals within two hours of schedule, while 33% were on or ahead of time. Easy servicing made for quick turnaround times, and the aircraft was popular with maintenance crews; but it was almost inevitable that the Comet, as with any new aircraft, would develop some teething troubles. During the first month of service mechanical faults caused delays amounting to nearly 40% of the journey time; but these were ironed out quickly, and eventually the figure bottomed out to 9%.

Although the Comet had captured the imagination of the public the world over and had clearly established a new benchmark in air travel, it would have been nothing more than a white elephant if it did not operate at a profit – and there were reports that BOAC was running the Comet fleet at a loss. Company chairman Sir Miles Thomas was quick to scotch these rumours, at the same pointing out that even if they had been true, the small fleet of Comets

**LEFT The Queen Mother is presented with a
bouquet on a royal visit to Hatfield with Princess
Margaret. Sir Geoffrey looks on fondly.**
(DH6329C/BAE Systems)

RIGHT **Your pint, sir. The elegant clothes, the muted pinks and blues of the passenger cabin, speak of an age gone by.** (Copyright unknown)

would still have provided invaluable experience in the new era of jet operation and thus would have been justified.

Research had shown that a load factor of 75% on BOAC's routes would realise a profit, but in their first year of operation Comets had averaged a load of 80%, and this resulted in enough profit to cover the interest of the capital outlay. Sir Miles was satisfied, and pointed out that the Comet had proved to be a mechanically sound aircraft capable of operating normally at unprecedented speeds.

By the end of the first year of Comet 1 service the 1A version was also operating, but neither series was ever envisaged as more than the starting point as far as de Havilland were concerned, and stretched versions with greater seating capacity and payload were well under way, the first being the Comet 2. Development work for this was carried out on a Comet 1 (G-ALYT) fitted with the more powerful axial flow Rolls-Royce Avon 502 engines. It was known as the Comet 2X.

While the Comet 1 and 1A were establishing their credentials worldwide, and proving a huge crowd-puller wherever they landed, the first production Comet 2 (G-AMXA) flew at Hatfield on 27 August 1953. Although only 3ft longer than its predecessors, the 2 was powered by two Avon 504 engines (inner nacelles) and two 524 engines (outer), each of 7,300lb thrust – almost half as much again as the Ghost. All-up weight increased to 120,000lb, payload from

CENTRE **Steady as a rock: you could build a house of cards in the Comet and it wouldn't collapse, so smooth was the aircraft. To be accurate, this particular one wouldn't collapse anyway, as it was a posed picture on the ground – but it was nevertheless a true portrayal of in-flight reality.** (DH5252/BAE Systems)

RIGHT **Another evocative picture to illustrate the comfort and relaxation of the new age of jet travel.** (Copyright unknown)

ABOVE A meeting of two forms of travel: four jet engines and four legs – and all of them firmly on the ground at Khartoum. The fourth production Comet (G-ALYU) and second to be delivered to BOAC was later used in the test tank at Farnborough in the ground-breaking accident investigation. *(British Airways)*

ABOVE Comet 1 (G-ALYW) being serviced and prepared for the next passenger schedule. *(N.D. Welch)*

RIGHT A touch of colour and glamour at Haneda Airport in 1952, where G-ALYP received a rapturous reception. *(DH74431/ BAE Systems)*

11,800lb to 13,500lb and still-air range from 1,770 to 2,535 miles.

With its greater capability and economic potential, this new version was very attractive to airlines, and by the time it was on flight trials 28 had been ordered, making a total of 47 Comets of all marks on order or delivered. The plan was to follow up with the Comet 3 for transatlantic operations, which would have a much longer fuselage and greater passenger capacity, as well as even more powerful Avons of 10,000lb thrust each.

At the end of 1953 de Havilland were ready to deliver the first Comet 2s to BOAC, who had revised their initial order for 14 Comet 1s to 9 Comet 1s and 12 Comet 2s. To speed up production, second and third assembly lines were set up at de Havilland's Chester factory, which had been producing Vampires and Venoms, and at Short Brothers' factory in Belfast.

South African Airways (SAA), who were interested in the Comet but had not yet committed to buying any, opened their Comet service on 4 October the same year with aircraft hired from BOAC, but sporting SAA livery and manned by South African crews.

By the close of 1953, orders for the Comet 2 were: BOAC, 12; Air France, 6; Panair do Brasil, 4; UAT, 3; Canadian Pacific, 3; British Commonwealth Pacific Airlines, 3; Linea Aeropostal Venezolana, 2; Japan Air Lines, 2. Orders had also been placed for the Comet 3: Ministry of Supply, 1 (G-ANLO); BOAC, 5; Pan American Airways, 3; Air India 2.

The Japanese order was placed within three months of the ratification of the Peace Treaty between Japan and the Allied Powers, and was part of their plan to expand from domestic services to routes outside the country.

But it was the Pan American order that was particularly significant, for it was evidence that America had been jolted out of its complacency; and Pan-Am made history by being the first American operator to order a front-line British airliner. America had been concentrating on developing better propeller-driven transports, believing that jet travel was some years away, and it was inconceivable to them that Britain could produce an operational jet airliner, brought to its knees as it was by the war. But once the Comet went into service,

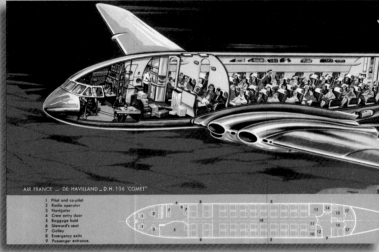

AIR FRANCE — DE HAVILLAND — D.H. 106 "COMET"

1 Pilot and co-pilot
2 Radio operator
3 Navigator
4 Crew entry door
5 Baggage hold
6 Steward's seat
7 Galley
8 Emergency exits
9 Passenger entrance.

THIS PAGE Some evocative pages from Air France's brochure on the Comet, extolling the advantages and simplicity of the jet airliner.

DE HAVILLAND "Comet"

★ 4 "GHOST" turbo-jets each giving 4,980 lbs. static thrust at take-off.

★ Fuel: kerosene (par).

★ Tank capacity: 7,040 gallons.

★ Maximum weight at take-off: 50 tons.

★ Maximum pay load: 12,200 lbs.

★ Maximum range with full pay load: 1,490 miles.

★ Maximum cruising speed: 460 miles per hour.

16

★ The total surface of the Comet is 2,012 square feet, which is roughly the equivalent of the surfaces of 5 single-deck buses.

★ Length overall ... 93 feet

★ Wingspan .... 114 feet 10"

★ Outside diameter . 11 feet 6"

The increasing speed of planes made it desirable to do away with propellers which, at very high speeds, brought about compressibility phenomena which increased drag and decreased lift. But was it possible to fly without a propeller?

The advances made in jet propulsion have shown that doing away with propellers brought about a definite improvement in commercial planes intended for use on certain lines.

Everyone knows that as a gun shoots its projectile, it recoils against the shoulder of the marksman. Hence it is possible to imagine a plane in which a number of machine guns have been set up pointing tailwise, the recoil furnishing the energy required for propulsion. A turbo-jet, is a tube inside which combustion followed by violent expansion takes place. The burned gases expelled backward furnish by jet reaction the forward thrust to the plane fitted with this tube. (A similar principle is used to operate revolving sprinklers).

The cockpit
The galley

CLASSIC...

The De Havilland "Comet", which opens a new era in aviation, retains the classic lines of aircraft which have long proved their worth on the air routes of the world. Yet it seems racier, more elegant than its predecessors, with its tapered, swept-back swallow wings, thickening at the roots for the oval air intakes of its four jets, its slim, sleek fuselage, tall fin and butterfly tailplane. The clever blend of modern techniques with time-proved methods has been crowned with resounding success. Slashing flying time by half, and radically changing the conditions of air travel, the Comet has risen magnificently to the confidence placed in its design.

SIMPLE...

In industry, most mechanical progress leads inevitably to increased complexity. The Comet's engines, however, mark a return to extreme simplicity. There are no pistons or valves, no connecting rods or crankshafts; the only moving parts are the compressor and turbine, rotating on the same shaft. The output of power is smooth, without jerk or surge. Even by placing the hand on the cowling of one of the jets, it is impossible to say whether it is working or switched off! It is evident that this simplification eases maintenance to a singular degree, and is a certain guarantee of reliability.

ABOVE **Air France's Comet 1A (F-BGNY) being serviced on 20 May 1953.**
(DH7040B/BAE Systems)

BELOW **A beautiful air-to-air shot of Air France's F-BGNX.**
(DH7065/BAE Systems)

American airline operators were forced to take an interest once they had recovered from their surprise – especially when they learned that BOAC was going to operate the Comet 2 on the South Atlantic route.

The wake-up call came from Wayne W. Parrish, editor of the magazine *American Aviation*: 'Whether we like it or not, the British are giving the USA a drubbing in jet transport. We've done our best to ignore their inroads on the prized world market, we've smugly acknowledged their valiant pioneering efforts, and we've thought up every sound, logical reason why we aren't prepared to have jet transports flying until 1958.'

The age of jet travel had arrived at the dawning of the new Elizabethan age, Britain had leapfrogged America by about five years, and the Comet was greeted with wonder and enthusiasm almost everywhere. Almost, but not quite: in spite of Parrish's forceful comments, there was one man who decided to see for himself how things were, rather than being told by someone else. That man was Trans World Airlines (TWA) vice-president Robert W. Rummel, and in October 1952 he visited

LEFT **UAT of France were an independent airline, and justifiably proud of their superb service with their two Comet 1As. Here is F-BGSA being serviced, while behind her is one of the two Comet 1As for Canadian Pacific Airlines.**
(DH6599C/BAE Systems)

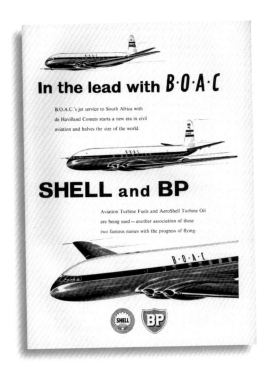

de Havilland on behalf of Howard Hughes. He wasn't overly impressed by what he found.

He thought the firm's tooling was rudimentary and that production was very slow. Compared with facilities in the States, this was obviously the case – although Rummel did acknowledge that the Comet was a superb pioneering achievement. However, he had reservations regarding the very thin fuselage skinning, the way everything had been pared down to save weight to achieve what he described as 'borderline performance', limited range and sluggish take-off performance at high angles of attack. He said the aircraft clearly needed more powerful engines.

Although he did not think any one of what he considered to be marginal conditions ruled the aircraft out, taken in combination they gave him 'pause for thought', and that was what he told Hughes, who accepted what he said. TWA criticised his judgement when they saw how popular the Comet was with fare-paying passengers, but time would show that Rummel's reservations had some foundation.

Rather in the way that America later tried to put noise objections in the path of Concorde, so the authorities tried to block the Comet by objecting to automatic certification. Although reciprocal certification had been agreed between Britain and America in 1944, with the advent of the Comet America decided this agreement held for piston engine aircraft only, and not jets. de Havilland were not happy.

After 18 months of service the Comet's reputation was intact – but not untarnished; for

ABOVE LEFT A Shell and BP advertisement to mark BOAC's Comet service to South Africa. The aircraft depicted in the centre has 'G-ALVG' on the fin, which was the first prototype and was not used on scheduled passenger flights.

ABOVE South African Airways' Comet 1a (G-ANAV) on hire from BOAC. *(DH7372A/BAE Systems)*

two weeks after Rummel's concerns about the aircraft's sluggish take-off performance, Comet G-ALYZ crashed at Rome's Ciampino Airport after failing to become airborne. Fortunately there were no casualties, but the aircraft was damaged beyond repair.

This was a serious blow to de Havilland, reeling as they were from the Farnborough disaster less than two months earlier when

BELOW Detail of the nose art on G-ANAV. *(DH7372C/BAE Systems)*

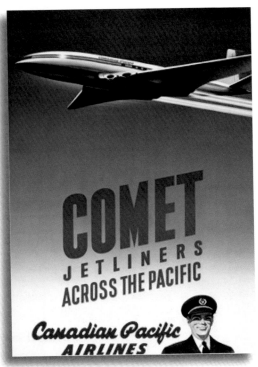

RIGHT Canadian Pacific's optimistic poster for their two Comet 1As. Sadly, things did not work out as they had hoped after the fatal take-off accident to CF-CUN.

OPPOSITE A fully fledged Comet 2 (G-AMXA) on her maiden flight. *(DH7241C/BAE Systems)*

their prototype DH110 all-weather fighter disintegrated in front of the vast air display crowd, killing not only famous test pilot John Derry and flight test observer Tony Richards but also 29 spectators, when one of the two Avon engines plummeted into a densely packed hill. A miscalculation on the strength of the outer part of the wing leading edge was later blamed.

Suddenly, instead of the media focusing on de Havilland's triumphal Comet, headlines the world over showed horrific images of a smoking engine on a crowded hill, a cockpit falling through the sky, a wrecked airframe lying on the airfield – and everywhere there was the name 'de Havilland'. It cast a huge cloud of despondency over the whole company.

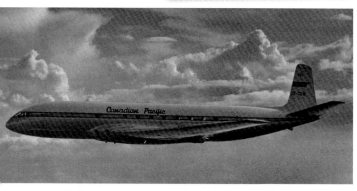

ABOVE One of Canadian Pacific's two Comet 1As (CF-CUN) against a sweeping skyscape. *(DH6481G/BAE Systems)*

BELOW A striking shot of the Comet 2X (G-ALYT) against a darkening Zurich sky in August 1953. *(Air News Service)*

ABOVE One of a pair of Comet 1As delivered to the Royal Canadian Air Force for transport duties. These were modified and strengthened after the Comet tragedies and went on to give many years of excellent and safe service. *(DHC2/BAE Systems)*

BELOW The following month G-ALYT was in Rio de Janeiro and greeted by enthusiastic crowds. *(Copyright unknown)*

COMET IN THE MOVIES

Two Comet 1s featured briefly in David Lean's award-winning film *The Sound Barrier*, which was released in July 1952. This is considered one of the finest aviation films ever made, combining stunning aerial photography around a story interwoven with fact and fiction, and displaying a sensitivity and lyricism that has eluded most other films of the genre.

As Tony Garthwaite (Nigel Patrick) and his wife Sue (Ann Todd) arrive by Vampire N113 (WP232) at Farouk Airport (now Cairo International Airport), they see the second production Comet (G-ALYR) parked on the apron. However, when they leave to fly back to England they are aboard the second prototype (G-ALZK).

All flying in the film was done by test pilots John Cunningham and John Derry from de Havilland; Mike Lithgow, Jeffrey Quill, Dave Morgan, Les Colquhoun and Gordon 'Chunky' Horne from Supermarine; and Trevor 'Wimpy' Wade of Hawkers. Along with the aircraft, they are featured in the opening credits. Wade died before the film premiered when the Hawker P1081 he was testing crashed, and Derry was to die two months after the film was released. These were dangerous times.

ABOVE While the David Lean film *The Sound Barrier* was proving a huge box office success in 1952, some of the team took a trip to Orly Airport. Pictured with a BOAC Comet are (left to right) Mike Lithgow, Supermarine chief test pilot; David Lean, producer and director of *The Sound Barrier*; Dave Morgan, Supermarine test pilot; Ann Todd, who starred in the film with Ralph Richardson; Neville Duke, Hawker chief test pilot – although he was not part of the production. *(Getty Images)*

Chapter Six

Comet accidents

The Comet, it seemed, could do no wrong and everything right. Tens of thousands of passengers were carried in speed, smoothness and luxury over millions of miles. The Comet basked in glory – but then came the accidents. Some were easily explained, but soon came shock and tragedy as two Comets disintegrated violently at high altitude with total loss of life. The love affair was over, but the investigation into the cause of the disasters established a template for all future crash analyses.

OPPOSITE **The ill-fated Canadian Pacific Comet 1A,** *Empress of Hawaii* **(CF-CUN). This was the first Comet to be in a fatal accident when all on board lost their lives after it crashed on take-off at Karachi.** *(BAE Systems)*

ABOVE Although this is a Comet 2 (G-AMXA), the picture illustrates the high angle of rotation available on take-off. With the tail bumper on the ground, and without a leading edge droop, the Comet 1 did not have enough power to overcome the huge drag caused by the wings at such an extreme attitude. *(DH8007A/BAE Systems)*

G-ALYZ

The take-off procedure for the Comet was different from piston engine aircraft and required greater diligence from the pilot. Without propellers, the only airflow over the wings was that generated by the speed of the aircraft itself, whereas propellers gave a good blast of fast-moving air over the wing and flaps which aided take-off performance.

If the Comet 1 wasn't exactly under-powered, it certainly didn't have much in the way of reserve power at take-off, and pilots were instructed not to allow the tail bumper to touch the runway during the procedure. 'At 80 knots the nose should be raised until the rumble of the nose wheel ceases' was the instruction in BOAC's Comet manual. 'Care should be taken not to overdo this and

adopt an exaggerated tail-down attitude with consequent poor acceleration.' However, this instruction is different from de Havilland's *Pilots' Notes* published in December 1951, which says: 'The nose wheel must not be raised from the runway until a speed is attained five knots below the unstick speed. The nose is then raised so that the aircraft leaves the ground at the unstick speed.'

If the nose was raised too high, the angle of attack generated more drag than the engines were able to overcome, the wing would stall and the aircraft would not be able to leave the ground.

It was raining on the night of 26 October 1952. Comet G-ALYZ, the second production aircraft, was on the routine London–Johannesburg service and was preparing to leave Ciampino Airport, which was one of the intermediate stops. The unfortunate captain on that day was 36-year-old Harry Foote. With 5,686 flying hours in his log, including time as an instructor on Avro Yorks, Lancastrians and Hermes, Foote was an experienced pilot.

As he lined up the Comet for take-off, all settings were correct with 15° flaps and engine rpm at 10,250. Visibility was about 5 miles, although no horizon was visible. At an airspeed of 75–80kt the nose wheel lifted off the ground, and at 112kt Foote eased the aircraft off the runway with a backward pull on the control column. As he called for 'undercarriage up' the port wing dropped violently and the aircraft swung to the left. Foote was able to regain level flight – but then noticed that speed was not building up and a pronounced buffeting set in.

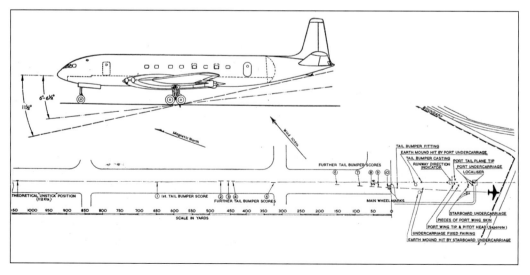

RIGHT Drawings from the report of the take-off accident at Rome, for which the pilot was blamed. *(Copyright unknown)*

Before the first officer could raise the undercarriage, the aircraft bounced down on its main wheels and Foote abandoned the take-off, realising the end of the runway was in sight and that G-ALYZ was never going to get airborne. The Comet hit a mound of earth and slithered for 270yd. When it came to rest, the main undercarriage had been ripped off, the port wing and tailplane had smashed into airport boundary lights and fuel was spilling from a ruptured wing tank. There was no fire and no one was injured, although everyone was badly shaken.

An investigation quickly revealed what had happened: the nose of the Comet had been raised too high and the tail bumper had hit the runway in a series of scrapes over 650yd. The accident report concluded that Foote had made an error of judgement in not appreciating the excessive nose-high attitude of the aircraft.

Sighs of relief all round: the Comet was not blamed – but Foote was, and was relegated to lumbering around in Avro Yorks once more. His fate was hotly disputed by the British Airline Pilots Association (BALPA), who cited the inconsistencies between the Comet Training Manual and de Havilland's Operations Manual. But it was to no avail, and many felt that Foote had been made the sacrificial lamb on the altar of the Comet. Nevertheless, a revised take-off technique was introduced: 'The nose wheel must not be raised from the runway until a speed is attained five knots below the unstick speed. The nose is then raised so that the aircraft leaves the ground at unstick speed' – exactly the words from the *Pilots' Notes*.

But this did not help Foote's case, and it wasn't until a similar, but more serious, accident happened a few months later that de Havilland decided to modify the wing leading edge to prevent further ground-stall incidents.

CF-CUN

On 3 March 1953 a Canadian Pacific Airlines (CPA) Comet 1A *Empress of Hawaii* (CF-CUN) was destroyed at Karachi Airport on its delivery flight. CPA Captain Charles Pentland, together with his co-pilot plus a crew of four and six passengers – including some de Havilland personnel – was to deliver the aircraft from London to Australia to take part in the trans-Pacific service.

A seasoned airline pilot, but with only ten hours on Comets, Pentland was planning to set an elapsed time record for the England to Australia route. He had been on the Comet conversion course at Hatfield, where Cunningham had personally instructed him on the revised take-off technique following Foote's accident. As Cunningham pulled the stick back and showed him exactly what Foote had done, Pentland was shocked: 'Holy Jeez,' he exclaimed, 'how on earth did the chap do that?'

A week later Pentland did exactly the same thing, this time with fatal results.

Take-off from Karachi was to be at 3am and would be the first Comet night flight by CPA crews. The aircraft was at maximum weight, with full tanks of fuel and some Comet spares on board. The horizon was obscured by ground haze.

As the take-off run progressed, CF-CUN was

ABOVE Canadian Pacific's Comet 1A *Empress of Hawaii* (CF-CUN) pictured at Hatfield, shortly before she was destroyed with total loss of life after failing to get airborne at Karachi Airport in March 1953. *(DH6727A/ BAE Systems)*

RIGHT The leading edge modification made on Comets following the two take-off accidents. The pronounced droop is evident on this view of a Comet 2 leading edge under construction. (DH9173A/BAE Systems)

seen to adopt a very nose-high attitude, and after the aircraft had used up the entire length of the runway its undercarriage hit a culvert on the perimeter drainage ditch. The aircraft crashed into a dry canal bed beyond the airfield boundary and immediately burst into flames. All on board died in the fierce blaze. Among them were chief de Havilland liaison engineer David Edwards, Comet flight engineers David Morgan-Tipp and Basil Rees, senior engineer Harold Waters (who had been on the maiden flight of the first prototype) and Ghost engine specialist John Wilson (not to be confused with de Havilland test pilot John Wilson).

As in the Rome incident, there was evidence of the tail bumper striking the runway. But, unlike the Rome incident, CF-CUN was at maximum take-off weight and the air was hotter

and thinner in Karachi.

As with Foote, Pentland was blamed. The inquiry concluded that 'the circumstances required strict adherence to the prescribed take-off technique, which was not complied with'. The findings were contested by the International Federation of Airline Pilots Associations (IFALPA), and six years later Pentland was cleared. The unfortunate Foote wasn't.

In spite of pilot error being the official cause of both accidents, the Comet's reputation had suffered and Canadian Pacific immediately cancelled orders for two further aircraft. de Havilland realised that take-off performance was a serious issue, and after further trials by Cunningham at Hatfield, Bishop redesigned the leading edge to incorporate a slight droop. This cured the problem completely and became a standard fitment, with only a very small penalty at high speed.

The symmetrical section of the Comet's wing was designed primarily for high Mach number performance, and the irony is that the prototype had originally been fitted with leading edge slats, which are a feature of all modern airliners and would have prevented both accidents. But in flight trials on the prototype they had little effect on stalling behaviour and, because of their complexity, were abandoned. However, with the drooped leading edge it was possible for a Comet to take off with the tail bumper scraping the runway.

G-ALYV

Almost to the hour of the first anniversary of jet passenger travel, and only two months after the Karachi incident, a BOAC Comet fell in pieces from the skies over India with complete loss of life.

On 2 May 1953 Captain Maurice Haddon, described by Cunningham as 'a splendid chap', had landed G-ALYV, the fourth Comet 1 delivered to BOAC, at Calcutta's Dum Dum Airport for refuelling. At about 4.20pm he was ready to take off for Delhi with a crew of 6 and 37 passengers, some of whom were headed for London to see the coronation of Queen Elizabeth II.It was the monsoon season, and there had been warnings of an approaching thunderstorm with 'very strong vertical updraughts', but after discussions with the

BELOW The memorial in Karachi to those who died on CF-CUN. (Copyright unknown)

THEY GAVE THEIR LIVES
IN THE
ADVANCEMENT OF FLIGHT.

IN MEMORIAM
CAPTAIN C.H.PENTLAND, CAPTAIN C.N.SAWLE, CHIEF NAVIGATOR P.D.ROY
RADIO NAVIGATOR J.R.COOKE, CHIEF ENGINEER J.A.SMITH
OF
CANADIAN PACIFIC AIR LINES, LIMITED
VANCOUVER CANADA.
D.H.EDWARDS, D.MORGAN-TIPP, B.W.H.REES, H.WATERS, J.A.B.WILSON
OF
DE HAVILLAND AIRCRAFT COMPANY

RIGHT The wreckage of G-ALYV near the paddy fields of Rangoon. Very little is recognisable here, but in the upper left of the picture next to one of the rice field workers is part of a Ghost engine with the combustion chambers, while among the luggage and mail bags in the foreground is – incongruously – the frame of an umbrella. *(Getty Images)*

weather office he did not feel a diversion was necessary.

The aircraft encountered heavy turbulence, but Haddon decided to fly on through the storm. At 4.53pm contact was lost when the aircraft was at an altitude of about 7,000ft, and workers in paddy fields near the village of Jagalogori about 24 miles from the airport heard a violent noise through the raging of the storm and saw wreckage, some of it burning, fall to the ground. An immediate search was launched, and the following morning the crash site was located by a BOAC Avro York, piloted in a strange twist of irony by Captain Harry Foote.

A public inquiry was set up under an Indian High Court judge, and the remains of G-ALYV were shipped to the RAE at Farnborough for examination. Every component was labelled and laid out like a giant jigsaw puzzle, then subjected to a highly detailed analysis. Scientists looked closely for any evidence of design weakness, but found none, and metal fatigue was not considered either as a cause or contributory factor. The break-up was thought to have originated from failure under excessive load of the port elevator spar.

The conclusion of the inquiry was that the Comet had suffered structural failure while flying through a thunderstorm, and the court's opinion was that this was caused either by severe gusts, over-controlling or loss of control by the pilot when flying through the storm. But it was only an opinion; no definitive cause was ever established.

The inquiry recommended stricter speed limits when flying through turbulence, but of greater significance was that the accident led to the installation of weather radar on all Comets. de Havilland disputed that over-controlling was likely to have caused the break-up. Cunningham was perfectly happy with everything as it was, and felt the Comet was a responsive aircraft.

Confident

In spite of these incidents BOAC remained confident in the Comet, and de Havilland press officer Martin Sharp commented that the accidents were easily explained and there was nothing mysterious about them. Comets were flying 177,000 miles a week and their record of safety and punctuality was satisfactory, de Havilland had set up a worldwide network of servicing facilities, jet travel was firmly established, and by the close of 1953 the Calcutta crash was viewed as a freak tragedy due to extreme weather conditions.

Although metal fatigue was not blamed for this accident, the phenomenon was very much the focus of the aviation industry on both sides of

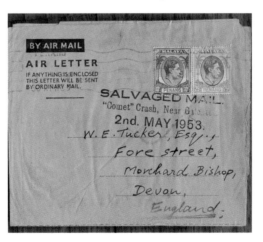

LEFT Among the mail on board G-ALYV was this letter to England, salvaged from the wreckage. *(Copyright unknown)*

DINKY TOYS COMET

It was unfortunate that by the time Dinky Toys produced a die cast model of the Comet in 1954 bearing the registration G-ALYV the real aircraft had crashed, but this did not affect sales and it was a great success with thousands of schoolboys. However, Meccano Ltd, who produced Dinky Toys, decided it was not in the best taste to continue with these markings and replaced it with G-ALYX in February 1956, when it joined the Dinky Supertoys catalogue with the model number changed from 702 to 999.

LEFT The Dinky Toys model of G-ALYV was popular, but as the aircraft it represented had crashed, a later version was released with the registration G-ALYX. *(Copyright unknown)*

BELOW G-ALYV, which was to be the first Comet to suffer an in-flight disintegration with total loss of life. It happened during a severe storm over Rangoon – but, unlike later accidents, happened at a comparatively low altitude, so decompression was not the prime suspect. *(Copyright unknown)*

the Atlantic in the early 1950s, as there had been crashes of various aircraft as a result of in-flight structural failure. Suddenly the realisation was dawning that aircraft did not have an unlimited life, that wings would weaken as the result of thousands of bending and twisting stresses from routine flying. The RAE were conducting tests, and made de Havilland and other aircraft manufacturers aware of these concerns.

de Havilland, meanwhile, had been continuing with static tests on Comet airframe specimens ever since the aircraft went into service, and G-ALVG was being subjected to a full-scale programme of fatigue tests. This did not mean that the Comet was rushed into service before sufficient testing had been carried out, as de Havilland felt totally confident from their pre-flight static test schedule that Comet airframes would last for many thousands of hours before the possibility of failure, and they had gone far beyond the statutory requirements of the time. Those tests were not for fatigue evaluation but to ensure the Comet hull was satisfactory as a pressure vessel.

The focus in Britain and America was primarily on the effects of metal fatigue on wings, as these seemed the most likely components to fail – and indeed they had failed on various aircraft.

The term 'metal fatigue' was nothing new, having been coined in 1850 by the steam engine pioneer James Braithwaite. Yet suddenly the aviation industry seemed to be taken by surprise that aircraft were beginning to fall apart, and the dangers of metal fatigue were not appreciated until 1952.

New regulations were introduced by the ARB in June 1953, which called for a static test to 2P (cabin pressure) and a proof test to 1.33P, but raised the number of applications of 1.25P to 15,000. Starting in July, de Havilland renewed their focus on the integrity of the cabin and carried out 18,000 pressurisation cycles on two full-scale test sections of the Comet 1

fuselage before there was a failure originating from a skin defect at the corner of a window; so it appeared that the Comet's fuselage was, in Bishop's words, 'built rather like a submarine, so that it would never fail' – at least not in the service life of the aircraft. At the start of these trials no Comet had flown for more than 2,500 hours, or about 800 pressurised flights, so there was not the slightest concern that a hull would fail for many thousands of hours.

But G-ALVG's wings were also undergoing rigorous stress testing in close cooperation with the RAE, and in December 1953 small cracks began to appear in the structure after the equivalent of 6,000 flying hours. None of BOAC's Comet fleet had flown anything like this much, but the unexpectedly low figure was worrying. No chances were taken, and regular inspections were scheduled so that remedial action could be carried out at the first sign of any problem. The question arose as to whether it might be necessary to withdraw Comets from service in a programme of wing modifications. This was not a palatable prospect, as it would inevitably tarnish the reputation of the aircraft – especially when viewed against the Calcutta crash.

But the decision never had to be taken, for less than three weeks later BOAC and the Comet were overtaken by a shocking tragedy.

G-ALYP

On the morning of 10 January 1954, G-ALYP, the very Comet that had famously inaugurated jet passenger travel, was at Rome-Ciampino Airport on a stop from the Singapore to London service. It had flown for a total of only 3,681 hours, including testing and training flights. Piloted by 31-year-old Captain Alan Gibson, DFC, with a crew of 6 and 29 passengers, and operating under the callsign Speedbird 781, G-ALYP took off at 9.31am in fine weather. The aircraft climbed quickly through thin, broken cloud and was soon at 26,000ft.

Crewing with Gibson were first officer William Bury, engineer officer Francis McDonald, radio officer Luke McMahon, steward Frank Saunders and air hostess Jean Evelyn Clark. Passengers were J.P. Hill, J. Steel, F.J. Greenhouse, R. Sawyer-Snelling (14), Captain R.V. Wolfson, Chester Wilmot, Mrs Dorothy Baker, H.E.

Schuchmann, Bernard Butler, Miss N. Khedouri (15) and Miss R. Khedouri (13), Mrs A. Bunyan and child, Mr and Mrs J.B. Crilly and child, Miss L. Yateen (17), Mrs K.E. Geldard, Miss G. Geldard and son, S. Naamin, Mrs E.S. MacLachlan, J.Y. Ramsden, Captain C.A .Livingstone (BEA captain), A. Crisp, Miss E. Fairbrother, Mr Israel, D. Leaver and T.S.H. Moore.

The best-known passenger was Chester Wilmot, an Australian war correspondent who was working for the BBC and had been part of the television commentary team for the coronation of Queen Elizabeth II. On the day of his death he was returning from an assignment in Australia where he had been narrating the story of recent royal visits.

As G-ALYP headed for London, Gibson radioed ATC to say he was climbing to 'cruising altitude 360' (36,000ft). Moments later he received a radio message from Captain J. Johnson who was piloting BOAC Argonaut G-ALHJ, which had taken off about 10min before the Comet: 'George Yoke Peter from George How Jig, understand you are passing 260; what's the cloud cover?'

Gibson radioed back: 'George How Jig from George Yoke Peter, did you get my …' The message broke off and no more was heard. The Comet would have been at about 27,000ft.

Very soon afterwards, fishermen off the west coast of Italy heard a series of shattering explosions and roaring noises, and looked up to see the dramatic spectacle of aircraft wreckage falling to the sea south of Cape Calamita near the island of Elba, some of it trailing flames and smoke.

An immediate search was set up, and about five hours after the accident 15 bodies were recovered from the water. Some had lost much of their clothing and were badly injured. No one could have survived such a horrific crash.

Sabotage suspected

After a conference in London headed by Sir Miles Thomas, chairman of BOAC, the corporation issued a statement saying that 'as a measure of prudence the normal Comet passenger services are being temporarily suspended'. This was to allow a thorough examination of every aircraft to be carried out at London Airport, and the decision was 'based on

ABOVE After the tragedy of G-ALYP a programme of modifications was carried out on all Comets in the hope of preventing another crash. Here technicians and fitters are at work on the wing of a BOAC Comet. *(Getty Images)*

BELOW Sir Miles Thomas, chairman of BOAC, announces to the press that Comet service will resume after modifications following the loss of G-ALYP. It was an ill-fated announcement. *(Copyright unknown)*

a desire to retain the good name of the Comet'. There was no government grounding order.

Speculation was rife, with sabotage being widely suspected. Or maybe it was fire; perhaps an engine turbine wheel shattering; possibly even clear air turbulence, as little was known at the time about the jet stream and the effect such high wind speeds might have on airframes. However, the instructions in the *Pilots' Notes* is to 'turn at right angles to the direction of the stream if this is possible', so the phenomenon was not entirely unknown.

The only certain way of finding out what had happened was for the wreckage to be retrieved, but this was a long and laborious task involving a number of vessels making sweeps up and down until they had covered 100 square miles. The water was between 360 and 600ft deep in this part of the Mediterranean, but fortunately the seabed was sandy, which allowed underwater television cameras to scan the wreckage and recover it with grabs and trawls – at least when the water was calm. As

Commander of the Mediterranean Fleet, Earl Mountbatten, put it: 'In the disturbed winter water, at five hundred feet, one is lucky if one can see ten feet, either by direct vision from the observation chamber or by underwater television cameras. The wreckage is spread far and wide, and is extremely difficult to locate. It is rather like searching for a handful of peas in a one-acre field from a helicopter on a misty day.'

On the day after the crash a group of experts was set up under Charles Abell, deputy operations director of BOAC engineering. It was known as the Abell Committee and included representatives from de Havilland, BOAC, the ARB and the Accidents Branch of the Ministry of Transport and Civil Aviation.

The prospect of keeping the Comet fleet grounded until the long process of recovering the wreckage was completed followed by an investigation was unthinkable, for it would take many months, and there was huge pressure to come up with an explanation. And so the committee decided to look at what they felt were all possible causes and make appropriate modifications to the Comets.

Medical examinations had ruled out sabotage, as there was no evidence of explosive residue on the bodies recovered. But there was strong evidence of explosive decompression injuries, although no indication at that stage as to what had caused disruption of the hull.

The committee discussed what they considered six possible causes of the crash: control surface flutter; primary structural failure caused by severe gusts at high altitude; failure of the flying controls; fatigue of the structure, particularly in the wing after cracks had shown up on a test specimen at the RAE unexpectedly early; explosive decompression of the cabin; or engine fire.

They did not suspect the cabin itself, but were concerned about possible defects in the window panels which might not have shown up during de Havilland's test programme. However, Bishop was positive that their 18,000 repeated loadings removed any doubt about failure originating within the hull, and Abell felt that wing failure was much more likely.

Modifications

In the absence of any conclusive evidence, and with pressure to resume passenger service, the

ABOVE With its long length hardly ideal for English roads, the fuselage of G-ALYU needed some driving skill to negotiate it round tight corners – and this was one of the tightest. *(DH7875H/BAE Systems)*

BELOW And it wasn't just the fuselage that had to be taken to Farnborough: equally tricky on narrow roads and sharp corners were the wings of G-ALYU. *(DH7876H/BAE Systems)*

A DIFFICULT JOURNEY

When all Comets were grounded after the second disaster off the Italian coast, G-ALYU had been sitting on the runway at London Airport about to take off. Instead, its passengers had to disembark and it never made another commercial flight. After returning to Hatfield it was taken by road to Farnborough to be tested to destruction in what was to become the most famous accident investigation of all time. These pictures illustrate what a tricky operation it was for Pickfords to take the fuselage and wings by road to Farnborough.

BELOW This view gives an idea of the scale of the task – and also the huge overhang of the fuselage from the rear of the flatbed. *(DH7875F/ BAE Systems)*

BELOW A sketch of G-ALYP. The shaded areas depict wreckage that was recovered from the sea. *(Copyright unknown)*

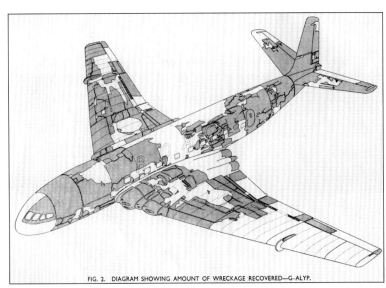

FIG. 2. DIAGRAM SHOWING AMOUNT OF WRECKAGE RECOVERED—G-ALYP.

committee decided on 50 modifications which they felt would cover all possible causes. Many of these were routine and would have been scheduled in over a period, but special attention was given to fitting armoured shielding between the engines and fuel tanks, as at the end of their deliberations the committee felt that fire was the most likely cause.

It was all guesswork, and nothing more than a scattergun approach had been made in the hope that at least one or some of the modifications would prevent further similar incidents.

Lord Brabazon wrote to Alan Lennox-Boyd, Minister for Transport and Civil Aviation, saying that modifications were being carried out to 'cover every possibility that imagination has suggested as a likely cause of the disaster'. This was followed up by Lennox-Boyd asking the Air Safety Board (ASB) for advice. In his reply on 5 March, Air Chief Marshal Sir Frederick Bowhill, ASB chairman, admitted the possibility that the Calcutta and Elba crashes might have a common factor, but that 'everything humanly possible had been done to ensure that the desired standard of safety shall be maintained. This being so, the Board sees no justification for imposing special restrictions on Comet aircraft.'

G-ALYY

But the ASB's decision, made on assumptions and guesswork, was a fatal one. Just two weeks after passenger service was resumed on 23 March another Comet was lost in an almost exact repeat of the Elba disaster – and, by coincidence, again after leaving Ciampino Airport. On Thursday 8 April G-ALYY, which was on charter to SAA from BOAC, took off from Rome on its way to Cairo with 7 crew and 14 passengers. It had been fitted with all the modifications stipulated by the Abell Committee, and with only 2,704 hours of flying time, had fewer hours in its log than G-ALYP.

It had been delayed for 24 hours at Rome because the central fuel tank contents gauge was not working. While fixing this, the engineer found 22 bolts lying loose in the port wing. An inspection panel between the rear spar and wheel well had not been replaced correctly, and another 30 bolts had not been done up tightly enough.

The South African crew was headed by Captain Wilhelm Mostert. With him were first officer Barent Grove, navigation officer A.E. Sissing, radio officer B.E. Webbstock, engineer officer A.R. Lagesen, air hostess P.L. Reitz and steward J.B. Kok. Passengers on this flight were O.L. Anderson, Mr and Mrs A.B. Brooks, Miss D.M. Eady, F.H. Harbison, M.A. Lamloum, Dr J. Stuart, R.L. Wilkinson, Miss N. Young, Captain J.A. Collings, J.F. Murray-White, E.S. Hack, J. Rosenburg and Mr Salzman.

Flying as SA201, G-ALYY took off late in the afternoon and climbed through three layers of moderately thick cloud. The last messages received were at 6.57pm, that it was climbing to 35,000ft, followed at 7.05pm, in which Cairo was told of the estimated arrival time. All attempts to make further radio contact failed, and the aircraft crashed off the coast of Sicily near Stromboli.

BELOW G-ALYY pictured in 1953, a few months before the disaster. *(Paul Zogg)*

As the water was between 520 and 580 fathoms deep, there was no question of being able to recover the wreckage. There was no need, for examination of six bodies pulled from the sea revealed the same kind of trauma as the Elba tragedy, and both aircraft had crashed under very similar circumstances.

The crashes came as a terrible blow to BOAC and to British aviation prestige. The pride of the fleet had fallen. Now there was no option but to take all Comets out of service, and their Certificate of Airworthiness was withdrawn on 12 April, just as BOAC Comet G-ALYU was preparing to take off from London Airport to Johannesburg at 3pm. It never left the runway. Next day the headlines said it all: 'Comet lost: all grounded'.

All production of Comet aircraft stopped, although development work on the Comet 3 continued, and de Havilland diverted men and tooling on to fulfilling orders for other aircraft. All Comets were flown back to London Airport by volunteer crews. The aircraft were lightly loaded and flown below 20,000ft. Two went to Hatfield for examination by de Havilland, and three others joined G-ALVG at Farnborough.

Investigation

There was no question this time of guessing what might have gone wrong; the cause had to be found, and Prime Minister Winston Churchill announced that 'the cost of solving the Comet mystery must be reckoned neither in money nor in manpower'.

An investigation was launched immediately, one that was to become a benchmark for future accident analyses. The Minister of Supply, Duncan Sandys, appointed RAE Director Sir Arnold Hall to lead the investigation. Hall was a brilliant scientist with a logical and organised mind, a kind of Sherlock Holmes of aviation mysteries.

The project had three objectives: flight tests on Comets to assess the structural integrity of the aircraft, particularly the cabin and the tail, and to investigate the possibility of control surface flutter; recovery of as much of the wreckage of Yoke Peter as possible for it to be reassembled at Farnborough; and the construction of a huge water tank to subject a complete Comet hull to repeated pressurisation loadings until failure occurred, and at the same time to carry out stress loadings on the wing.

Wreckage recovery operations off Elba were intensified while construction of the water tank began. At 112ft long, 20ft wide and 16ft high, it was a massive engineering task, yet was completed in just six weeks, with teams of men working round the clock, and by early June G-ALYU was immersed in the tank with its wings projecting from the sides. Although de Havilland had done their own exhaustive water tank tests before and after the Comet went into service, the RAE project had two crucial differences: first, de Havilland had never tested a complete hull – only sections – and, second, those sections were not entirely representative of production units, as the windows had been Redux bonded, whereas on production Comets punch rivets were used for the window frames.

The RAE test, with a complete production Comet and wings, would be able to simulate as near as possible real-world conditions of repeated pressurised flights. The cabin was subjected to thousands of cycles of pressure while the wings were constantly flexed with hydraulic rams to give the typical loadings experienced in flight. One problem was not only how to make a watertight seal around the wings, but for keeping the seal watertight while the wings were being moved up and down. The solution was a special inflatable tube.

As the Elba and Stromboli crashes appeared to happen near the top of the climb to cruising altitude, the RAE decided that flight tests under these conditions were necessary to see if they revealed events that could lead to an explosion or loss of control. Sir Arnold was

ABOVE Wreckage recovery from the Mediterranean was a massive and painstaking operation. Here a large part of G-ALYP is hauled from the seabed.
(Copyright unknown)

ABOVE The massive
water tank at
Farnborough with
G-ALYU undergoing
fuselage pressure
tests and
wing loadings.
(Crown copyright)

ABOVE RIGHT
Flexible seals around
the wings prevented
water escaping
from the tank when
loads were applied.
(Copyright unknown)

very concerned at subjecting flight crews to
what were clearly very risky trials from which
there could be no escape in the event of
disintegration – but there was no other way.
However, it was decided not to pressurise
the cabin, but to issue the crews with oxygen
masks instead: the idea was not to risk an
explosive decompression but to observe any
abnormalities with controls, behaviour of the
aircraft or anything else unexpected.

Comet G-ANAV, which had flown for 1,255
hours, was chosen for the trials and was fitted
out with extensive test equipment, including
strain gauges and vibration sensors after all the
passenger seats and fittings were removed. In
effect, it was a flying laboratory that in addition
to the flight crew would carry RAE scientists to
monitor the equipment.

The first of 50 exploratory flights was made
on 23 June, each one shadowed by a Canberra
bomber to observe any unusual behaviour and
warn the crew if necessary. Nothing dramatic
happened and no clue arose as to what might

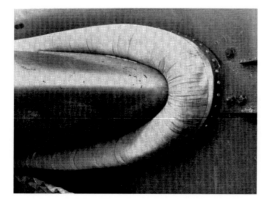

RIGHT A close-up of
the inflatable
wing seals.
(Copyright unknown)

have happened to YP or YY – but the aircraft
did not exactly come away with a clean bill of
health. The pilots found a disconcerting lag
between movement of the control column and
the aircraft's response, and at altitude there was
a tendency to move the column in jerks and
to over-correct. They also found a tendency to
float just before touching down, and the rudder
was not effective at low speeds in a crosswind.

Small cracks

While these flights were going on, close
watch was kept on the water tank as the
pressurisation cycles continued day and night.
The first component to show signs of failure
was the wing, which was not unexpected. Small
cracks were visible around the undercarriage
bays, but although of concern, these were not
thought to be the origin of the crashes, and
once they were repaired the testing went on.

As the flight tests and tank tests continued,
more and more wreckage was arriving from
Italy, and the salvage crews were having greater
success than initially expected. In charge of
collating all the pieces and assembling them on
a full-size wooden framework of the Comet was
Eric Ripley, principal scientific officer of the RAE
structures department. But so far there was
nothing conclusive to indicate what had caused
the disaster.

The first breakthrough came on 24 June in
the water tank. From time to time, as a proving
test, the cabin was pressurised to 11lb/sq in
instead of the usual 8¼. On that day, just before
it reached the target figure, the cabin burst.

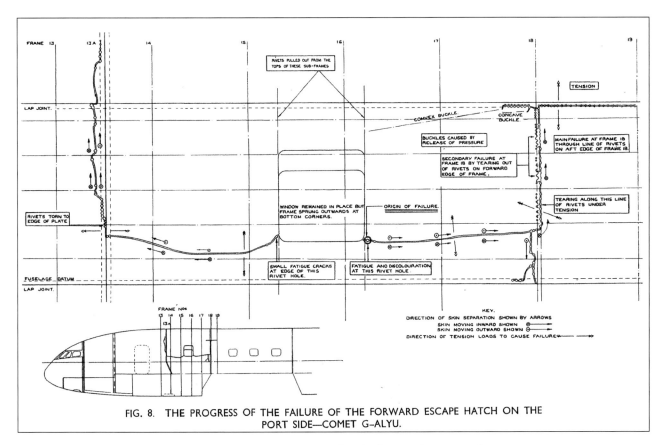

FIG. 8. THE PROGRESS OF THE FAILURE OF THE FORWARD ESCAPE HATCH ON THE PORT SIDE—COMET G-ALYU.

Sir Geoffrey de Havilland and Bishop were immediately called and scrutinised the damage themselves. There was a rent 8ft long and 3ft wide over the port wing, and metallurgists confirmed that it was caused by metal fatigue originating from a rivet hole at the corner of the escape hatch. There was another smaller fatigue crack 1¼in long at the corner of a window on the port side over the wing.

These failures occurred after the equivalent of 9,000 flying hours, which was far more than Yoke Peter or Yoke Yoke had done before they crashed – in the case of YY, three times more. But there was no way to predict a precise

ABOVE Diagram showing the path of skin failure on G-ALYU in the Farnborough water tank. *(Crown copyright)*

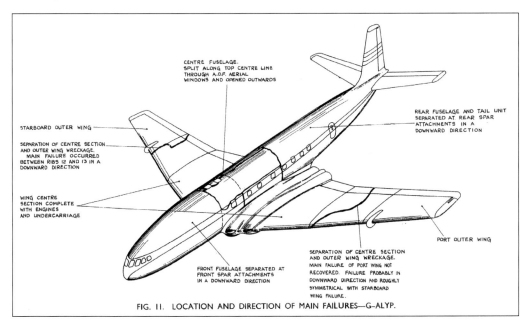

FIG. II. LOCATION AND DIRECTION OF MAIN FAILURES—G-ALYP.

LEFT A sketch of G-ALYP showing the main points of break-up. *(Crown copyright)*

RIGHT Impact
damage to G-ALYP's
upper wing surfaces.
(Crown copyright)

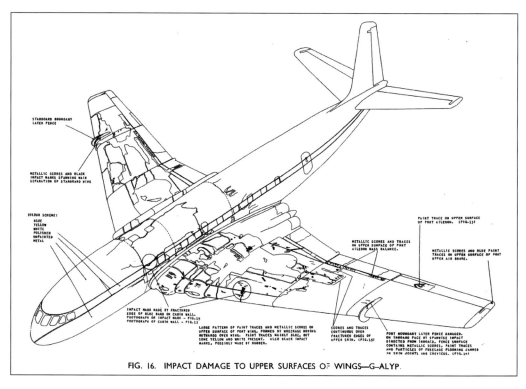

FIG. 16. IMPACT DAMAGE TO UPPER SURFACES OF WINGS—G-ALYP.

BELOW A chaotic blur
of dummies and seats
when a scale model
of the Comet fuselage
was subjected
to an explosive
decompression at
Farnborough. It gave
a graphic depiction
of what it must have
been like inside
G-ALYP and G-ALYY
within half a second
of the fuselage failing.
(Copyright unknown)

lifespan before metals failed owing to fatigue.
An average figure could be arrived at, but in
practice failure could occur at a third of that
average or three times beyond it, so the figure
of 9,000 was within these limits.

But it was still not positive proof of what
caused the crashes: until the relevant pieces of
wreckage were found, those that had evidence
of fatigue failure, no conclusion could be drawn.
All four engines had been recovered more or
less intact when the wing centre section was
pulled from the sea on 15 March, and had been
cleared of blame after a complete strip-down
and thorough examination. However, damage

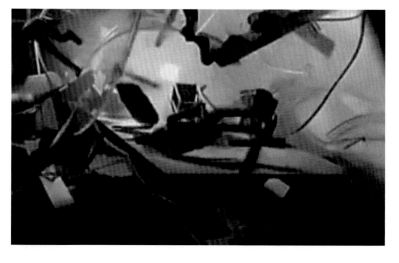

common to all four Ghosts indicated a sudden
and catastrophic downward rotation of the whole
wing while the engines were running normally.

As the investigation progressed, and Ripley
painstakingly put his giant Comet jigsaw
together as more and more wreckage arrived
at Farnborough, an explosive decompression of
the cabin became the prime suspect – especially
when paint marks from the fuselage were detected
on the inboard section of the wing, small pieces
of carpet from the passenger cabin were found
in the tail section and the imprint of a coin was
visible on a rear fuselage panel. But this still did
not prove that the cabin was the first part to fail:
the disintegration could have started in the outer
part of the wing and cabin failure could have been
secondary; so it was vital that these sections were
found. Eventually they were, and faint marks were
discovered on the aileron and near the boundary
layer wing fence on the port wing. Under analysis,
these were found to be from the cabin, thus
proving conclusively that the hull was the first
component to fail. But still that vital piece was
missing, the piece that could hold the key, which
would have evidence of a fatigue failure.

Models

Early in the investigation more than 50 small
wooden flying models of the Comet were made,

each with a wingspan of about 3ft. The main objective was to get an idea of the likely spread and pattern of the Elba wreckage to help the salvage teams narrow down their search – especially for the vital outer parts of the wings.

From his jigsaw, Ripley soon had enough evidence to deduce the likely sequence of break-up, and the models were designed to come apart in the air in a similar way. This was achieved by launching them by catapult from the top of a tall hangar, a cord attached to pins inside the model causing a sequential disintegration. Further and more accurate tests were done from a tethered balloon and the

results were filmed as the models fell apart. When everything was analysed and scaled up, the results were remarkably accurate.

What would happen inside the Comet's cabin if there was an explosive decompression? Sir Arnold resorted to the methodology of models once again. A one-tenth scale Comet cabin was constructed at the RAE out of Perspex and the interior was fitted with bulkheads and 28 miniature seats with six dummy passengers, all scaled to the correct size and weight as much as possible. The model was placed in a pressure chamber and high-speed cine cameras were set up to record the event.

ABOVE Piece by piece, the remains of G-ALYP's fuselage are assembled on a fuselage framework at Farnborough. *(Crown copyright)*

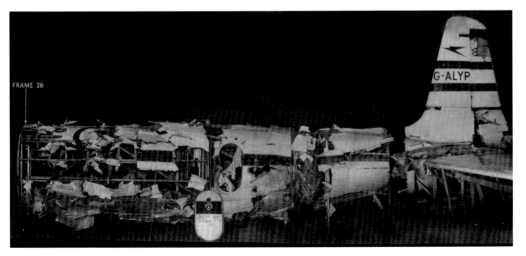

LEFT With great skill and patience, Eric Ripley assembled all the available pieces of G-ALYP like a giant jigsaw – a jigsaw that was to tell a story. *(Crown copyright)*

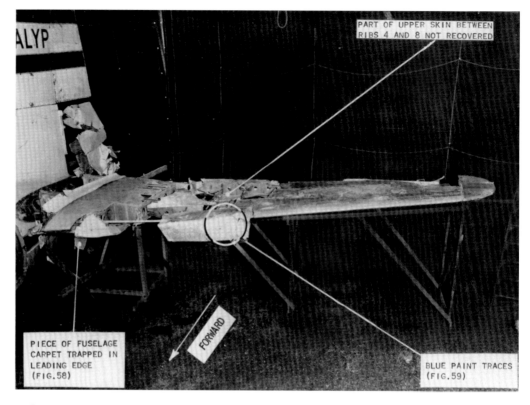

RIGHT A close-up of G-ALYP's port tailplane. Points highlighted show where a piece of carpet was trapped and where traces of blue paint from the fuselage were found. *(Copyright unknown)*

PART OF UPPER SKIN BETWEEN RIBS 4 AND 8 NOT RECOVERED

FORWARD

PIECE OF FUSELAGE CARPET TRAPPED IN LEADING EDGE (FIG.58)

BLUE PAINT TRACES (FIG.59)

BELOW The rupture to G-ALYU's hull in the test tank. It came as a shocking surprise to de Havilland. *(Crown copyright)*

BELOW RIGHT A close-up of the point of failure. *(Crown copyright)*

The pressure in the chamber was reduced until it was equivalent to an altitude of 40,000ft. At the same time the pressure in the hull was increased to 8½lb/sq in. Conditions were now those of a Comet at cruising height. The plan was to simulate a rupture by the sudden removal of a small plastic seal attached by cables to an electrical bomb release mechanism.

The result was one of shockingly sudden chaos. In 0.03sec the seat-backs in the aft end of the cabin were moving forward; after 0.1sec complete chaos had broken out; and after 0.7sec seats were flying about in all directions, one dummy passenger hitting the roof with great violence while other bodies and seats hurtled through the rupture.

At least the end for those in YP and YY would have been so quick that they would have known absolutely nothing: one minute all was well and less than a second later they were all dead, with no warning whatsoever of their fate.

ORIGIN OF FAILURE

ORIGIN OF FAILURE

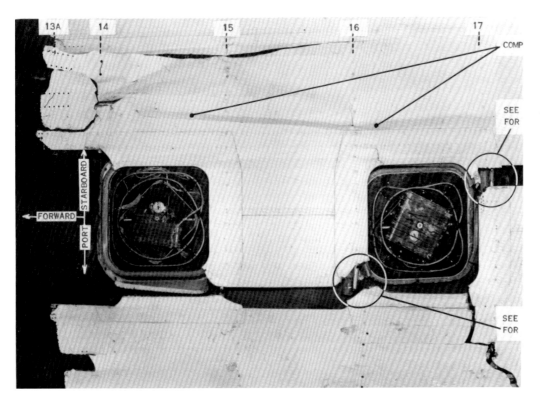

LEFT The fuselage splits that brought down G-ALYP – right on the vulnerable radiused corners of the ADF windows. *(Copyright unknown)*

BELOW A close up of the rear ADF window, with cracks on all four corners. *(Copyright unknown)*

Confirmation

The pattern of disintegration, the water tank test on YU, the Perspex model's explosive disruption: all pointed to a violent decompression originating in the hull, but still the final proof eluded the investigators, the piece that held the definitive answer. Then, on 12 August, with almost three-quarters of Yoke Peter's wreckage recovered, the section of the hull that Ripley had been waiting for arrived at Farnborough – plucked from the seabed not by the salvage vessels, which had been told to sweep a wider area in the hope of finding it, but by an Italian fishing boat, although its significance was not realised until it was scrutinised at Farnborough.

It was an area of fuselage roof above the wings that housed the ADF square fibreglass apertures. Although often referred to as windows, they were not for looking through but to prevent electricity being conducted through the metal of the hull. After a cursory examination, Ripley knew he had found what he was looking for: there were cracks running from the rear ADF window across the skin of the fuselage, and detailed examination showed irrefutable evidence of metal fatigue around a bolt hole.

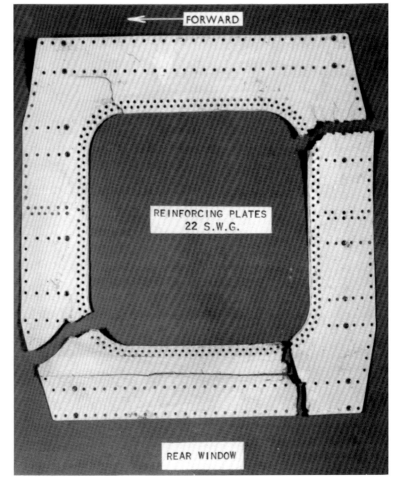

FORWARD

REINFORCING PLATES
22 S.W.G.

REAR WINDOW

For Sir Arnold and the dedicated team of scientists the job was done. The evidence was conclusive, and the salvage operation was terminated in September after seven months of remarkable success. Now there were detailed reports to compile for the forthcoming public inquiry. So labour intensive had the investigation been, that Sir Arnold said many of the staff involved had been working 80hr weeks – and some as much as 100 to 120 hours a week to solve the mystery as quickly as possible. 'I drove my staff, and incidentally myself, well beyond normal limits,' he said. It had been an extraordinary undertaking, the most extensive accident investigation the world had ever seen.

The inquiry

In spite of de Havilland's extensive testing and absolute conviction that the hull would never fail in the service life of the aircraft, two Comets had suffered a catastrophic explosive decompression very early in their career. Why? The public inquiry would reveal all.

When the court opened at Westminster on 19 October 1954, Sir Lionel Heald QC, appearing on behalf of the Crown, told the assembly that the investigation by Sir Arnold and his team was 'one of the most remarkable pieces of scientific detective work ever done'.

The principal witness was Sir Arnold, and he described in detail the findings of the RAE investigation. Referring to the experiments with Comet G-ALYU in the water tank at Farnborough, he said that when failure occurred near the forward escape hatch the structure at that point had a peak stress of 45,700lb/sq in, and it was deduced that such stress was reached two or three times per flight. The ultimate static strength of the material was about 65,000lb/sq in, so that failure occurred at 70% of the ultimate.

Sir Arnold said the degree of stress concentration at the forward escape hatch was the same as that at the ADF window, although the two structures were different. 'We examined the fractures in the area of the rear ADF window of G-ALYP which we had already decided was the origin of the failure, and we found what we

BELOW Details of the pressure hull's failure.
(Crown copyright)

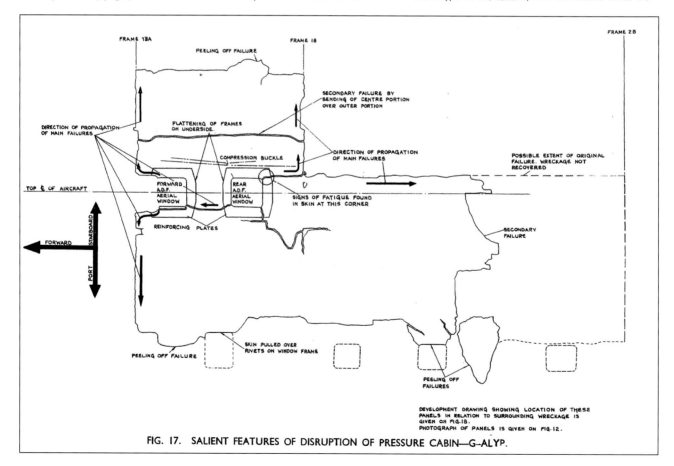

FIG. 17. SALIENT FEATURES OF DISRUPTION OF PRESSURE CABIN—G-ALYP.

believe to be evidence of high-level fatigue at one particular point.'

Chief structural engineer of de Havilland, Bob Harper, disagreed with Sir Arnold's peak stress figure – in fact there was considerable disagreement between them on a number of matters in the early stages of the inquiry, but this was mainly because of different interpretations of calculations and tests, and as the inquiry progressed there was a better understanding between them. For example, Sir Arnold's figure of 45,700lb/sq in contrasted wildly with de Havilland's 28,000lb/sq in, but was explained by the fact that the RAE figure related to a specific point at the window, whereas the de Havilland estimate was taken over an area of several inches.

Chief designer Bishop told the court that cabin differential pressure was one of the biggest problems they had to face. 'We were very alive to the consequences of a failure,' he said. 'It was quite obvious right from the start that if the structure of the pressure cabin failed or if a window blew out at 40,000ft, it was at least a very serious situation, and a great deal of thought and testing was done with the object of making sure that the pressure cabin was safe. We obviously missed the main point.'

Evidence of a romantic rather than scientific nature was given by Lord Brabazon, chairman of the ARB. He attributed the Elba crash to 'the adventurous pioneering spirit of our race. It has been like that in the past, it is like that in the present, and I hope it will be in the future.'

But the real reason was that de Havilland's extensive tests had been conducted in ignorance of the nature of metal fatigue in the conditions under which the Comet would be operating. The cabin had failed much earlier than they had expected, and the stresses had been much higher at specific points than they had believed. There were several reasons for this.

First, they had not subjected a complete fuselage to repeated loadings – only sections, one of which was 26ft long, the other 24ft. These were provided with stiff bulkheads at each end, which would lead to stress readings different from a production hull – and neither section was fitted with a complete number of windows. Moreover, the windows on the front test section were positioned near the bulkhead, so the stresses on

the skin around them would not be representative of a complete fuselage. Unlike production Comets, the windows in the test specimens were Reduxed in place. This method was going to be used on production Comets, but in practice caused considerable difficulty so rivets were used instead. But these were punch rivets, which are much more brutal to the metal than riveting through pre-drilled holes, and they can cause minute stress cracks around the holes which have the potential to propagate.

The fuselage of YU in the RAE test tank failed much earlier than de Havilland's test specimens, and Sir Arnold believed this could be because de Havilland's 1953 tests were carried out on a nose section that had previously been preloaded to a pressure of 16½lb/sq in – or 2P – and this could give extra strength to the structure by altering its properties. Harper told the inquiry he was aware of that possibility, but he felt that their tests more than covered the life of the aircraft.

At the end of the inquiry de Havilland were cleared of blame, and Lord Cohen concluded that they had followed well-established procedures and adhered to what were considered throughout the industry to be sound engineering principles.

But there was a recommendation that de Havilland should modify the Comet's flying control system to reduce the break-out force of the control column and to give the pilot a more positive feel of loads exerted on the control surfaces.

So at the end of an inquiry which produced a report 10in thick, no one was blamed for anything – not even the ARB for resuming Comet passenger flights before the mystery of the Elba crash had been solved. But some good came out of the tragedies: new light was shed on the dangers of metal fatigue and, in particular, the design and static testing of pressure hulls. de Havilland never tried to hide anything, and the inquiry and its conclusions were made available to the aviation industry worldwide.

The task facing de Havilland was now to make the appropriate modifications to the Comet fleet and rebuild its reputation. But it never happened. No one wanted to fly on the Comet any more, and no Comet 1 or 1A ever carried fare-paying passengers again.

But the story of the Comet was far from over.

Chapter Seven

Rebirth of the Comet

Although it could never recapture the Comet 1's glory days of 1952, the design was basically sound, and in the form of the Series 4 rose Phoenix-like from the ashes and went on to give many years of safe service with airlines throughout the world. It also inaugurated the first transatlantic jet passenger service, narrowly beating the Americans with their Boeing 707.

OPPOSITE BOAC's Comet 4 (G-APDR) displays her beauty as she banks away from the camera. *(DH12201A/BAE Systems)*

ABOVE Re-skinning the fuselages and fitting circular windows to Comet fuselages at the Broughton plant following the accident inquiry. *(Philip J. Birtles collection)*

Although all Comet 1 production was stopped at Hatfield after the tragedy of Yoke Yoke, and the firm was reeling in disbelief, other Comet development continued in the form of the stretched Comet 3 designed for the transatlantic route. The prototype (G-ANLO), which turned out to be the only Series 3 example built but with which much of the development work for the definitive Comet 4 was done, first flew from Hatfield on 19 July 1954 and logged enough hours to be demonstrated at the Farnborough Air Display in September. This sent out a bold message: the Comet may be down, but it is not out.

However, there was serious fallout from the accidents as orders were cancelled. A vast

Comet production line at Short Brothers in Belfast was shut down with little more than two fuselages built, 30 airframes in the pipeline at Chester were cancelled, as were seven more at Hatfield. The loss to de Havilland on the manufacturing side alone was about £10 million – equivalent to around £250 million 60 years later – and Britain's lead in jet travel was no longer unassailable, as America was able to incorporate knowledge gained from the disasters in their ground-breaking Boeing 707. The forerunner of the 707, the 367-80, known as the Dash 80, had first flown four days before G-ANLO and was initially developed as a transport and flight refuelling tanker, only later being considered for civil operation.

Meanwhile, as the Comet investigation progressed, de Havilland were saddled with 25 Comet 2s in various stages of completion. They faced the strong possibility that the whole batch would be scrapped, but when the results of the investigation and inquiry were published it was clear that all the faults of the Comet 1 could be eliminated, mainly by using thicker 19swg fuselage skinning instead of the very thin 22 gauge, and by fitting circular windows, which would give an even stress distribution, as opposed to the dangerous concentration of stresses at the corners of square windows.

Several Comet 1s had been destroyed during the RAE investigation, and the remaining samples were taken over by the government for experimental purposes after their seats and other internal fittings were removed – the aircraft were considered too valuable to be scrapped. And in March 1955 the Comet 2 airframes were passed to the Ministry of Supply, who announced that 15 of them would be flown: ten for RAF Transport Command, three for RAF special duties and two for further development with BOAC. The civil pair were known as the Comet 2E and were powered by two Rolls-Royce Avon 504s in the inner nacelles and Avon 524s in the outers.

LEFT A Comet 2, formerly G-AMXB, undergoing a fuselage rebuild at Hatfield in May 1955. It first flew on 9 December that year after being fitted out as a trainer for the RAF and bearing the serial XK669. *(DH8693A/BAE Systems)*

Strengthened fuselage

The fuselages were strengthened and the original square windows were replaced with rounded ones similar to the Comet 3. This was a major operation involving the substitution of the complete window panel with a much stronger one that had special reinforcements around all cut-outs, windows, hatches, doors and any other panel. This extended the safe operating life to more than 10,000 hours. Three other Comet 2s were completed as a fleet reserve, but they were neither used nor flown. The special duties trio (G-AMXA, XC, XE) were flown to Marshalls at Cambridge in the summer of 1955 for conversion to radio countermeasures duties with 192 Squadron, emerging with new serials XK655, XK659 and XK663. These three retained their original square windows and were flown unpressurised. Their task was the highly secret gathering of intelligence on the frequencies of hostile radars and weapon systems, and their cabins were packed with special avionics. They began operations with 192 Squadron in 1957, which was renumbered 51 Squadron the following year.

Meanwhile, the two Comet 1As of the RCAF were flown to England by John Cunningham and underwent similar conversion work. These flights were done at about 25,000ft to avoid using full cabin pressure, and when the aircraft were returned they went on to give many years of good service.

Air France's Comet 1As were flown back to Hatfield for modifications. With strengthened fuselages and oval windows, they became known as the 1XB. The third of these, F-BGNZ, flew again with the serial G-APAS – later XM823 – and after serving with the RAF and various trials programmes, it finally went to the RAF Museum at Cosford, where it is on view as a complete aircraft.

The first Comet to enter RAF service was XK670, which was delivered to 216 Squadron at Lyneham in Wiltshire on 7 July 1956 and joined by XK669. Designated the Comet T2, these sported orange dayglo bands on the nose and tail and were used for crew training before being joined by eight Comet 2Cs, which

ABOVE Comet C2 of 216 Squadron at Hatfield. *(Philip J. Birtles collection)*

BELOW Comet T2 (XK669) of 216 Squadron. *(Crown copyright)*

ABOVE **Comet C2
(XK671) of
216 Squadron.**
(DH9748F/BAE Systems)

were equipped with 44 seats and employed on transport duties, thus becoming the first jets to be used by the RAF in this role, and making history as 216 became the world's first squadron to use jet transports.

The Comet 2 had undergone the most rigorous testing before entering service and, in view of the troubled history of the Series 1, the decision was taken that it must obtain a full passenger-carrying Certificate of Airworthiness – unique for an RAF aircraft, but no one was taking any chances. Testing on two airframes had been done at Hatfield for structural strength and fatigue, and these showed that the aircraft would have a life well beyond what it would undergo in military service. The beefed-up fuselage structure added some weight, which was amply compensated for by the Roll-Royce Avon 114 engines, each producing 7,350lb thrust.

Proving flights were made to Aden in September 1956 and to Singapore in October, with Malta and Cyprus regularly on the schedule. The first operational flight by 216 Squadron's Comets was on 23 June 1956 when the Secretary of State for Air, Nigel Birch, was flown to Moscow at the invitation of Russian Prime Minister Nikolai Bulganin for the Soviet Air Force Day celebrations at Tushino Airport the following day. This was the first time a British jet had visited Moscow, and the trip was covered in four hours.

The Comet 2 set new records for an RAF military transport, including Lyneham to Adelaide in 38 hours. Its speed and versatility made it invaluable, not just in its transport duties

but in conflict zones worldwide, including Suez and Cyprus, as well as supporting V-bomber deployments. It also played a role during the missile trials at Woomera in South Australia and in the H-bomb tests at Christmas Island in the Pacific. A once-a-week Christmas Island service, via San Francisco and Honolulu, began on a regular basis in October 1957, and the 19,000-mile round trip involved a flying time of 45hr 30min.

That same speed and versatility made the Comet 2 ideal as an airborne ambulance for casualty evacuation (Casevac), and it was capable of carrying 36 patients with a combination of stretchers, reclining seats and standard troop-carrying seats, depending on the degree of their injuries or illness. Its ability to cruise in the calm conditions of 40,000ft meant there was far less discomfort for the seriously injured, and the journey time from, for example, Singapore to Lyneham was two days compared to the seven days with propeller-driven aircraft. At the other extreme, the Comet could easily be converted into a VIP transport, and it was used frequently for ferrying high-ranking officials, government ministers and members of the Royal Family.

The three Comet 2s that went into service with the original square windows, and therefore flew unpressurised, were delivered to 51 Squadron at RAF Wyton in 1957 and were equipped for electronic intelligence gathering (SIG/ELINT). Eventually the squadron would operate seven of these aircraft, designated Comet R2 and powered by Rolls-Royce Avon

506s producing 7,330lb thrust. They took over the spy role from the ageing Avro Lincoln and Boeing B-29A Washington.

Comet 3

The Comet 3, design work on which was well advanced by the time the Comet 1 made the world's first commercial jet passenger flight in May 1952, had oval windows from the outset and was a very different aircraft from the early Comets. It was 18ft 6in longer and would be able to carry 78 tourist-class passengers, or 58 first-class. Assembled in the Experimental Department at Hatfield, this super-Comet would be powered by four Rolls-Royce Avon 502 engines each developing 10,000lb thrust which, with a maximum take-off weight of 145,000lb, would give it a cruising speed of 500mph. Overhaul interval was 1,000hr. Additional fuel

ABOVE The Comet 3 (G-ANLO) is rolled out on 5 May 1954. Comet 2 (G-AMXC) is in the background. *(DH7857N/BAE Systems)*

ROLLS-ROYCE AVON

One of the most famous jet engines ever produced, the axial flow Avon was designed as a successor to the wartime Merlin piston engine and a replacement for the centrifugal flow Rolls-Royce Nene. With a diameter of 35.7in, it was 17in slimmer than the Ghost, so installation in the Comet presented no difficulties.

The design team was headed by Cyril Lovesey, the man behind the Merlin, and the first prototypes were built in 1947. The original configuration featured only a single spool, but this quickly progressed to a multi-stage compressor, and the first Avons to take to the sky were a pair of RA2s in a converted Avro Lancastrian (VM732) on 15 August 1948, and displayed at the Farnborough Air Show the following month.

There was such strong demand for the Avon from military and civil customers that it was produced at several plants and production was subcontracted to the Bristol and Napier engine companies, as well as the Standard Motor Company. It powered the Vickers Valiant (the first of the three V-bombers) the Hawker Hunter, the Supermarine Swift and the de Havilland DH110. On the civil front, it was fitted to the Sud-Ouest Caravelle twin-jet airliner as well as the Comet 4.

LEFT The Comet 3 about to have one of its Avon engines installed. *(DH10034/BAE Systems)*

Boeing 707 came along. The Comet was not designed to compete with American designs, but to complement them and optimise BOAC's passenger services.

The corporation took on two Comet 2Es (G-AMXD and XK) to gain early experience of the new Avon engines and to use them on route-proving trials between London, Beirut and Calcutta in preparation for the Comet 4. In June 1958 G-AMXK was used in an intense series of transatlantic proving flights spread over three phases, the first of which was 11 one-day return flights to Gander via Keflavik in Iceland. This was followed by eight three-day trips, starting with a flight to Gander on day one, Gander to Goose on day two, then on to Stephenville, Sydney and Moncton, before returning to Gander and then back to London. The Comet 2E logged 3,850 hours with BOAC, of which the Atlantic flights accounted for 423.

Meanwhile, Cunningham was busy with flight trials on the Comet 3. Although it had oval windows it did not have the new fuselage structure and was not fully pressurised, thus limiting its altitude to 20,000ft; but this did not compromise its long test programme as a proving vehicle for the Comet 4, which outwardly it closely resembled.

There was no better way to introduce this

ABOVE Against a towering backdrop of cumulus, the Comet 3 on a test flight. *(DH10191Z/BAE Systems)*

capacity was carried in the distinctive pinion tanks on the outer wing, replacing the boundary layer fences of earlier series.

BOAC had earlier ordered five Comet 3s, but cancelled everything until the outcome of the inquiry. Once the verdict was published, and it was clear that Comets could be built to the new standard of strength and fatigue resistance, a £34 million order was placed for the forthcoming Comet 4, which was seen as the ideal vehicle for all their routes, and could even be used on the north Atlantic schedule until larger American aircraft such as the

RIGHT A nice aerial shot of Comet 2E (G-AMXD) with the Comet 3 shortly before the Farnborough Air Show of 1954. XD was one of a pair of Comet 2Es that BOAC used for familiarisation of the Avon engines and route-proving trials in readiness for the Comet 4. *(DH8086R/ BAE Systems)*

new Comet to the world than to take it on a global tour, so on 2 December 1955, with G-ANLO sporting BOAC livery, Cunningham took off from a foggy Hatfield, set course for Cairo, followed by flights to Bombay, Singapore, Darwin and Sydney, which was reached in a flying time of 24hr 24min. Second pilot was Peter Buggé, while others on board included senior de Havilland and BOAC personnel. Next stop on the schedule was New Zealand, Fiji and Honolulu, followed by a flight across the Pacific to Vancouver, and on to Toronto and Montreal. Cunningham then flew G-ANLO home across the North Atlantic direct to Heathrow, arriving on 28 December after covering the 3,350 nautical miles in 6hr 8min, which was less than half the time of the fastest piston engine airliners. The aircraft had performed faultlessly throughout its epic journey.

Cunningham and the Comet received a rapturous reception wherever they went, and the sight of this beautiful aircraft, which looked even sleeker than the Series 1, coupled with Cunningham's ambassadorial qualities, did much to pave the way for the Comet 4's success. Opportunities were taken wherever possible to give demonstration flights to the press and airline personnel.

Over the years numerous myths had

circulated about runways not being long enough for large jet airliners, that the engine noise would be deafening and that there were dangers of being seriously burned by standing within 100yd of an engine that was running. Cunningham and the Comet 3 disproved these fanciful stories, and the sight of a fully loaded Comet pulling up into a climb far steeper than

ABOVE The Comet 3 created huge interest at the 1955 Farnborough Air Show. It was clear to all that the Comet was about to be back in business. (DFH8929K/ BAE Systems)

BELOW The Comet 3 (G-ANLO) rests on the runway at Essendon, Melbourne, Australia, on 8 December 1955. This was one of many stops on John Cunningham's ambassadorial global tour to put the Comet back on the map. (Copyright unknown)

ABOVE On a stopover for refuelling at Bombay, the Comet 3 takes a break during Its flag-waving global tour in December 1955.
(Copyright unknown)

any propeller type could manage left an indelible impression. Its short take-off and low landing speed surprised and impressed everyone, and it was capable of operating out of the world's major airports with no runway modifications.

Although G-ANLO was the only Comet 3 to fly, there was one other airframe at Hatfield, which was used for structural and cabin-pressure testing, and also for interior layout and design for the Comet 4. Before being broken up in August 1966, it was used for some initial Nimrod development.

Having done its job for de Havilland and BOAC, G-ANLO remained at de Havilland for

SHAKING ALL OVER

Brian Clarkson's first flight in a jet was in the Comet 3 – and it was not a pleasant experience. His speciality in the Structures Department at de Havilland was vibration analysis, and one day while working quietly in his office he became aware of someone sitting at the corner of his desk. To his surprise it was his boyhood hero, chief test pilot John Cunningham.

'I understand you're our vibrations expert,' said Cunningham, and then invited Brian to accompany him on a stall test in the Comet 3, where something odd had been happening.

At about 10,000ft Cunningham eased back the throttles until the airflow broke away and the aircraft began to fall like a brick. As it stalled, the whole fuselage began to vibrate at a very low frequency that caused Cunningham's head to nod and his body to bend in a bizarre and uncomfortable way.

Once he recovered from the stall, all was peace and quiet once more.

Investigations by Brian and senior de Havilland aerodynamicist John Wimpenny revealed that very low frequency wing vortices – somewhere between 4 and 8Hz – were hitting the tailplane and exciting a matching resonance in the fuselage. But the fuselage wasn't the only thing to start shaking: the natural frequency of a person sitting down is 6.3Hz, so Cunningham's body joined in the fun as well. This coupled response caused his head to nod and his body to keep bending backwards and forwards.

The remedy was quite simple, and involved decoupling one of the modal frequencies and stiffening the fuselage with a thick plate. The result was that the stall was much more comfortable, and this modification was incorporated in the production Comet 4.

conversion to B specification, with shorter wings and without its distinctive pinion tanks. After that, it passed to the Ministry of Supply under a new registration, XP915. It became one of four aircraft types used at the Blind Landing Experimental Unit (BLEU) at RAE Bedford in June 1961. In 1964, it was used to evaluate the Comet as a potential replacement for Avro Shackletons, used by RAF Coastal Command.

Comet 4

The safe operating life of the modified Comet 2 was more than 10,000 hours. The requirement for the Comet 4 was much greater – no less than 30,000 hours – and this meant that all components had to be tested to around five times this value. This was unprecedented, but for an airliner costing about £1 million in the 1950s it had to have a long life to make it an attractive economical proposition.

de Havilland had to build a new water tank for pressure testing the fuselage as well as the means of transmitting wing loads to the fuselage that represented take-off, landing and in-flight stresses. The fuselage test specimens were subjected to 120,000 pressurisation

ABOVE Known as 'Spike' for reasons that are obvious in this photograph, the Comet 3 was converted to B specification for trials work with the Blind Landing Experimental Unit (BLEU). *(PRM Aviation)*

cycles, which was equivalent to 480,000 flying hours, while the wing spars and root joints gave lives beyond 180,000 hours.

Finally, a complete aircraft was installed in the tank and testing began on 15 June 1958. The equivalent of a 4hr flight was completed every 2min, and consisted of applying stresses to the

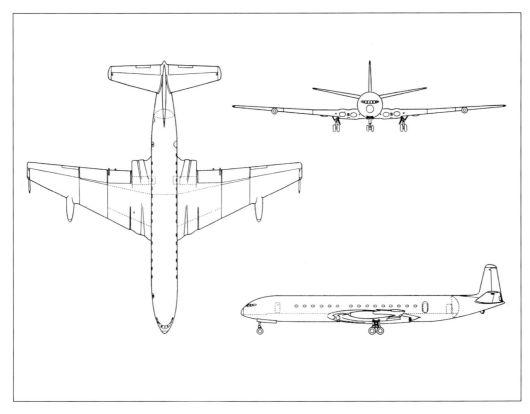

LEFT This general arrangement drawing of the Comet 4 shows how the jet-pipes are angled outwards to divert the hot gasses from the rear fuselage. *(Copyright unknown)*

de Havilland Comet 4. *(Mike Badrocke)*

1 Radome
2 Radar scanner
3 Front pressure bulkhead
4 Windscreen framing
5 Windscreen wipers
6 Instrument panel coaming
7 DME aerial
8 Rudder pedals
9 Cockpit roof construction
10 Co-pilot's seat
11 Control column
12 Pilot's seat
13 Engineer's control panel
14 Emergency escape hatch
15 Radio rack
16 Engineer's work table
17 Engineer's swivelling seat
18 Navigators' seats
19 Navigator's worktable
20 Nosewheel bay construction
21 Nosewheel leg strut
22 Twin nosewheels
23 Nosewheel door
24 Crew entry door
25 Crew's wardrobe
26 Forward galley
27 Galley supplies stowage
   boxes
28 Radio and electrical
   equipment bay
29 Forward starboard toilet
   compartment
30 Forward port toilet
   compartment
31 Wash basin
32 Air conditioning duct
33 Toilet servicing panel
34 Cabin window panel
35 First class cabin seats
36 Twin ADF loop aerials
37 Air conditioning grilles
38 Floor beams
39 Forward freight and luggage
   hold
40 Freight hold door
41 Control cable runs
42 Fuselage keel construction
43 Overhead hat rack
44 Cabin dividing bulkhead
45 Air distribution duct

46 Emergency escape window
47 Air conditioning plant
48 Hydraulics bay
49 Starboard wing integral fuel
   tanks
50 Flow spoilers
51 External fuel tank
52 Tank bumper
53 Fixed slot
54 Outer wing fuel tanks
55 Navigation light
56 Wing tip fuel vent
57 Static dischargers
58 Starboard aileron
59 Aileron tab
60 Flap outer section
61 Airbrake (upper and lower
   surfaces)
62 Fuel dump pipes
63 Fuel vent
64 Flap inboard section
65 Inboard airbrake (upper
   surface only)
66 Fuselage frame and stringer
   construction
67 Wing centre section fuel cells
68 Emergency escape hatch
69 Aileron servo controls
70 Main fuselage frame
71 Aft tourist class cabin
72 Rear freight hold/luggage
   compartment
73 Floor beam construction
74 HF aerial cable (port and
   starboard)
75 Overhead hat rack
76 Tourist class cabin seats
77 Aft galley
78 Starboard service door

79 Aft starboard toilet
   compartment
80 Aft radio rack
81 Rear pressure bulkhead
82 Anti-collision light
83 Dorsal fin fairing
84 Starboard tailplane
85 ILS aerial
86 Starboard elevator
87 Leading edge de-icing ducts
88 Fin construction
89 HF blade aerial
90 Rudder balance weight
91 Rudder
92 Elevator hinge controls
93 Elevator tab
94 Port elevator
95 Tailplane construction
96 ILS aerial
97 Leading edge de-icing
98 Tailplane attachment
99 Fuselage fin frame

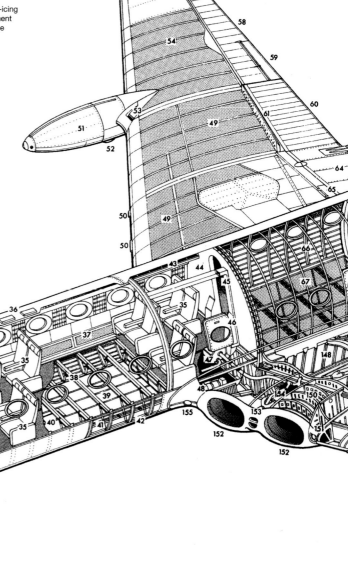

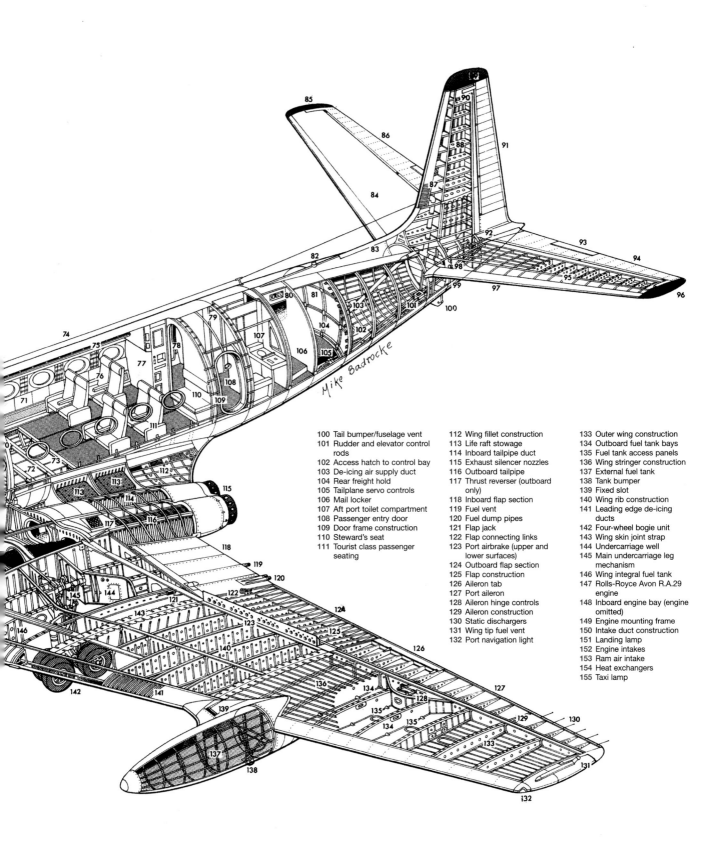

100 Tail bumper/fuselage vent
101 Rudder and elevator control rods
102 Access hatch to control bay
103 De-icing air supply duct
104 Rear freight hold
105 Tailplane servo controls
106 Mail locker
107 Aft port toilet compartment
108 Passenger entry door
109 Door frame construction
110 Steward's seat
111 Tourist class passenger seating
112 Wing fillet construction
113 Life raft stowage
114 Inboard tailpipe duct
115 Exhaust silencer nozzles
116 Outboard tailpipe
117 Thrust reverser (outboard only)
118 Inboard flap section
119 Fuel vent
120 Fuel dump pipes
121 Flap jack
122 Flap connecting links
123 Port airbrake (upper and lower surfaces)
124 Outboard flap section
125 Flap construction
126 Aileron tab
127 Port aileron
128 Aileron hinge controls
129 Aileron construction
130 Static dischargers
131 Wing tip fuel vent
132 Port navigation light
133 Outer wing construction
134 Outboard fuel tank bays
135 Fuel tank access panels
136 Wing stringer construction
137 External fuel tank
138 Tank bumper
139 Fixed slot
140 Wing rib construction
141 Leading edge de-icing ducts
142 Four-wheel bogie unit
143 Wing skin joint strap
144 Undercarriage well
145 Main undercarriage leg mechanism
146 Wing integral fuel tank
147 Rolls-Royce Avon R.A.29 engine
148 Inboard engine bay (engine omitted)
149 Engine mounting frame
150 Intake duct construction
151 Landing lamp
152 Engine intakes
153 Ram air intake
154 Heat exchangers
155 Taxi lamp

RIGHT Comet 4
(LV-PLM) of
Aerolineas Argentinas
on a proving flight.
(DH11857E/BAE Systems)

BELOW The one that
never happened: the
Comet 5, even more
graceful than the
Series 4. It would have
been powered by
four Rolls-Royce
Conway engines.
(DH9416/BAE Systems)

ABOVE **Flight deck of the Comet 4.**
(Copyright unknown)

RIGHT **Flight engineer's station on the Comet 4.**
(DH8070A/BAE Systems)

BELOW **The galley of an Aerolineas Argentinas
Comet 4** *(BAE Systems)*

COMET 4 POWER CONTROLS

The Comet 4 had power-operated ailerons, elevator and rudder, all of which had mass balances. The Comet 1 was criticised for its high stick force break-out and lack of feel, so the Series 4 had feelback provided by springs which gave an increasing load at the pilot's hands as the control surface deflected – although on the ailerons and rudder this was not directly related to airspeed. The elevator was different in that it used a q-feel device which gave increasing control loads with both deflection and airspeed, as well as a lower break-out force than the Series 1.

There were two schools of thought on the best control system for aircraft of this size and performance, and the Boeing 707, which was said to handle beautifully throughout its speed range, used old-fashioned manual controls throughout, apart from the spoilers – and that was merely to ease the pilot's workload. Even the variable-incidence tailplane was operated manually. With the 707 and the B-52 bomber, Boeing found that, even with all-up weights of more than 400,000lb and Mach numbers of up to 0.96, cable-operated manual systems did the job for which they were designed. They were rugged, reliable and had a natural feel to the pilot.

However, they did fall short at the lower end of the speed range, and to counteract this Boeing fitted an extra set of ailerons on the 707 to make up in area what was lacking in airflow. On the Douglas DC-8, which also used manual controls, power was added to the ailerons for low-speed operation to give extra displacement.

The famous test pilot Captain Eric 'Winkle' Brown flew the Comet 4 and, although he found it handled well, he was not over-impressed by its power controls. 'They felt lumpy,' he said. 'And yet I recall a power control system fitted experimentally to a Lancaster sometime earlier that was absolutely delightful.'

The system was certainly a contrast to the lightness and lack of feel of the Comet 1. Andrew Clarke, a flight lieutenant with 216 Squadron at Lyneham in the early 1970s, recalled that the controls were very heavy: 'You needed two hands all the time,' he said, 'but I never heard anyone complain. The aircraft handled beautifully, and was delightful to fly. The landing performance was superb: you just set it up and it would virtually land itself.'

Clarke, who was in his early 20s at the time, had plenty of experience on the aircraft, and during his tenure with 'Two-sixteen' made a total of four round-the-world trips carrying VIPs, which was one of the C4's main duties. He recalled a somewhat embarrassing moment: 'On one occasion we arrived to a brass band and line of dignitaries who had presupposed we would have our own internal stairway, like modern executive jets. After some minutes of keen anticipation and various national anthems, a set of rickety old maintenance steps arrived and the Air Chief Marshal and his wife in full regalia struggled down them with as much dignity as they could muster!'

ABOVE A Comet 4 thrust reverser. *(DH11020C/ BAE Systems)*

wing and fuselage encountered during a typical flight, including wind gusts, landing loads and cabin pressure. The tests continued up to the equivalent of 120,000 flying hours without failure.

Most of the flying development for the Series 4 had been done on G-ANLO, and when Cunningham took the first of BOAC's 19 aircraft (G-APDA) on its maiden flight on 27 April 1958, there wasn't a great deal of further testing to be carried out before it was handed over to the corporation for crew training – and, again, much of that had been accomplished on the Comet 2Es.

Pilots would find the Comet 4 flight deck significantly different from early Comets, with an improved layout, redesigned instruments and a new navigational suite. The nose radome housed an EKCO E160 radar unit that incorporated search functions as well as ground and cloud mapping capabilities.

A few months later, in August, G-APDA visited New York and managed to satisfy the very stringent noise regulations of the Port of New York Authority before departing for Hong Kong as part of the 100hr overseas flight requirements for ARB certification. The return trip of 7,925 miles to Hatfield was made in the record time of 18hr 22min with refuelling stops at Bombay and Cairo. To use up the rest of the mandatory overseas flying time, Cunningham flew around Canada, Central and South America, and home via New York. The 23,254 miles were covered in a flying time of 49hr 44min, an average of 468mph.

On 30 September, three days after G-APDA's return, two Comet 4s (G-APDB and G-APDC) were delivered to BOAC and on 4 October the two aircraft opened the world's first scheduled jet passenger service across the Atlantic. G-APDC took off from London Airport with Captain Roy Millichap at the controls, and at the same time DB left New York piloted by Captain Tom Stoney. The Comet was back – and it was still the Comet, in spite of suggestions that it should be renamed.

Sir Geoffrey was very much against that: 'It seemed to me to be like a clumsy sort of cheating,' 'he wrote, 'and would do more harm than good. It would be known sooner or later that we had deceived by a not very clever trick, and it was far better to prove that Comet failure was to be turned into Comet success.'

Not happy

The Americans were not happy: they had been pipped to the post on the Atlantic route by an aircraft that had been developed from a design that had blasted apart in mid-air three times. Now here were these British upstarts doing it again, and the best that America could do was launch their transatlantic service three weeks later, on 26 October, with the Boeing 707. But the magnificent 707 was the shape of things to come, and set the format for jet airliner design up to the present day: sharply swept wings and low-slung engines in pods.

In spite of the arrival of the Boeing jet which, depending on the version, could carry up to 179 passengers and had a cruising speed of 550mph, the Comet remained popular well into the mid-1960s and beyond, gave exceptional service, and was also the first jet airliner to operate in Latin America.

With their fleet of 20 Comet 4s, BOAC were able to span the world and operated across six continents, with services to 36 countries and 46 cities. There was no denying that the Comet was back – this time bigger, better and safer – and de Havilland received orders from airlines the world over. Unfortunately, America

was not one of them – although it almost was. In 1956 Capital Airlines had placed an order for four Comet 4s and ten Comet 4As after concluding that these were the ideal aircraft for Capital's operations; and the plan had been for them to go into service on their major and most competitive routes. However, Capital was taken over by United Airlines after running into financial difficulties, and the order was cancelled. It would have been worth £19 million.

ABOVE An Avon 502 engine about to be installed in Comet 4 (LV-POZ) for Aerolineas Argentinas. *(DH12569F/BAE Systems)*

BELOW Hull pressure tests and flight load simulations on the Comet 4 went on round the clock at de Havilland. The water tank was very similar to the one used at Farnborough for the accident investigation. *(DH11691A/BAE Systems)*

RIGHT **Celebrating the excitement and future of jet travel: an evocative front cover of *Flight* magazine, 6 February 1959.** *(Flight)*

6 FEBRUARY 1959

ONE SHILLING & SIXPENCE

FLIGHT

Aircraft, Spacecraft, Missiles

COMET 4

BY DE HAVILLAND AND ROLLS-ROYCE

The jet that is a known quantity — it will go everywhere and pay its way

Principal civilian operators of the Comet 4

Argentina: Aerolineas Argentinas ordered six Comet 4s in 1958, which were delivered in 1959, and on 16 April 1959 launched the first jet airliner service in South America between Buenos Aires and Santiago, Chile. On 19 May they introduced the first jet passenger service across the south Atlantic to Europe, and then in June opened the first jet link between North and South America with services to New York. Unfortunately, three of their Comets were involved in accidents: LV-AHP crashed several miles from Silvio Pettirossi International Airport on final approach, killing one passenger and one crew member; LV-AHO suffered a hard landing at Ezeiza Airport during a training flight; and LV-AHR collided with some eucalyptus trees on climb-out from Viracopos-Campinas International Airport and crashed. Owing to the

COMET 4 VARIANTS

COMET 4: First version to go into service with BOAC. Wingspan 114ft 10in, length 111ft 6in, maximum seating capacity 81. Fuel capacity: 8,990gal. Stage-lengths up to 3,000 miles. Payload 16,800lb. Payload accommodation: de luxe-class sleeperettes at 56in seat pitch, four abreast, 40 seats; first class – 40in pitch, four abreast, 56 seats; tourist class – 40in pitch, five abreast, 71 seats; economy class – 34in pitch, five abreast, 81 seats. Various mixed-class layouts were possible, typical being 24 first class at the front and 43 tourist class aft. A total of 19 were built.

COMET 4A: Planned specifically for the American market on internal routes, it would sacrifice fuel capacity for extra seating and would have shorter wings to reduce drag at lower altitudes. After the Capital Airlines order was cancelled, this version was never built.

COMET 4B: A short-haul version with lower cruising altitude than the 4, the 4B had an extra 7ft added to the fuselage giving a seating capacity of 101, and the wingspan

shortened by the same amount. It was the European equivalent of the 4A and could cruise at 530mph at 23,500ft. Fuel capacity: 7,890gal (the 4B did not have the wing nacelle tanks or wingtip tankage). Payload accommodation: first-class – 37in pitch, four abreast, 72 seats; tourist class – 34in pitch, five abreast, 102 seats. A total of 18 were built.

COMET 4C: With the wingspan of the 4 and the lengthened fuselage of the 4B, this variant's extra capacity made it very popular with a number of airlines, particularly in the Middle East. A total of 23 were built.

COMET 5: Proposed as an improvement over previous models, including a wider fuselage with five-abreast seating, a wing with greater sweep, a swept tailplane, Rolls-Royce Conway engines each developing 16,000lb thrust and a cruising speed of 560mph. Without support from the Ministry of Transport, the proposal was never realised.

loss of these aircraft, a replacement Comet 4C was bought in 1962. After being moved from international flights to domestic flights from 1966, the survivors were retired and sold to Dan-Air in 1971. Aerolineas Argentinas' last fatal accident was in 1970, and it remains one of the world's safest airlines.

Australia: Qantas leased seven Comet 4s in the early 1960s, mainly to operate the Sydney to Singapore route. At first these were to supplement their Boeing 707s, but the leasing arrangement was short-lived, as it wasn't long before the 707 took over completely.

East Africa: East African Airways operated out of the then British territories of Kenya, Uganda, Tanganyika and Zanzibar. They had two new Comet 4s delivered in 1960 and

another in 1962. Four other Comet 4s were leased from BOAC in the 1960s. These aircraft had no trouble operating from high altitude or hot airports and allowed EAA to reach an 11hr per day service. They expanded routes beyond Africa into Europe and India, and after a successful decade of operation their last Comet flight was on 19 February 1971.

Ecuador: AREA Ecuador had one Comet 4 delivered in 1966 that was used on services between Quito and Miami. In 1968, the aircraft was impounded at Miami as the result of legal action, and remained there until scrapped in 1978.

Egypt: The national airline of Egypt, Misrair, had two new Comet 4Cs delivered in 1960 to serve their extensive network of services over the Middle East, Europe and North Africa. The

ABOVE Lunch being served on a BOAC Comet 4 in October 1958 – still the same personal service as on the Comet 1 six years earlier. (DH12302K/ BAE Systems)

ABOVE LEFT

Photographed on the same flight: the ladies' dressing room. (BOAC)

FAR LEFT The latter stages of assembly on Comet 4 G-APDE at Chester in August 1958. (DH11423E/BAE Systems)

LEFT Another view of G-APDE. Just visible behind her is the nose of G-APDH. (DH11423B/ BAE Systems)

ABOVE She's almost finished: the men at the Chester plant who put her together pose proudly for the camera on 1 September 1958. *(DH11568D/BAE Systems)*

LEFT The fuselage of BOAC's Comet 4 G-APDC is towed out of the hangar for a final pressure test before further assembly. *(DH10749H/BAE Systems)*

airline, which became United Arab Airlines in 1961, took delivery of seven more Comet 4Cs over the course of the 1960s. Upon the transformation of United Arab Airlines into EgyptAir in 1971, four of these aircraft were inherited by the new airline and continued to give good service, mixing with Boeing 707s and Russian airliners. The Comets were sold to Dan-Air over the course of the 1970s.

Greece: The country's national airline, Olympic Airways, which was owned by the Greek shipowner Aristotle Onassis, leased two Comets from BEA in 1960 and operated them in a pool arrangement before acquiring four

LEFT History is about to be made as G-APDC prepares to take off from London Airport for the first scheduled transatlantic jet passenger service on 4 October 1958. *(British Airways)*)

Comets of their own. Onassis did not want to be left behind in the jet age, especially as BOAC and BEA were picking up most of the business.

Kuwait: Kuwait Airways was the last airline customer for the Comet and operated two Comet 4Cs in the 1960s, the main objective being to gain jet experience before taking delivery of the new Trident in 1966. The airline continued to use the Comet alongside the Trident, but this did not get off to a good start, the second one crashing after one month's service.

Lebanon: Middle East Airlines (MEA) purchased four Comet 4Cs in 1960, with an option on a fifth, to open a service from their Beirut base to London, Frankfurt, Athens and Bombay, with other Asian and European destinations in the pipeline. The option on the fifth aircraft was not taken up, and although it was demonstrated in MEA livery at the Farnborough Air Show in 1961, it was sold to Aerolineas Argentinas as their only 4C after their loss of three Comet 4s. MEA continued Comet operations in spite of a worsening political situation in the Middle East, but faced a serious setback when three of their Comets were destroyed on the ground by an Israeli commando attack in December 1968. With only one Comet remaining, they leased a 4C from Kuwait Airways and kept the service going until

1971, when they sold their Comet to Dan-Air who purchased it for spares.

Malaysia: Malaysian Airways initially leased Comets from BOAC until they purchased five second-hand Comet 4s in the 1960s. The airline became Malaysia–Singapore Airlines in 1966 and their Comet fleet served numerous destinations in the Far East, as well as Perth

ABOVE Taking off at the same time as G-APDC so that they would cross halfway over the Atlantic, G-APDB gets airborne from New York Idlewild.
(Copyright unknown)

LEFT 'You arrive gloriously fresh, hardly realising you've travelled at all!' BOAC trumpeted the virtues of long-distance jet travel when they launched their Comet 4 service to the Far East.
(British Airways)

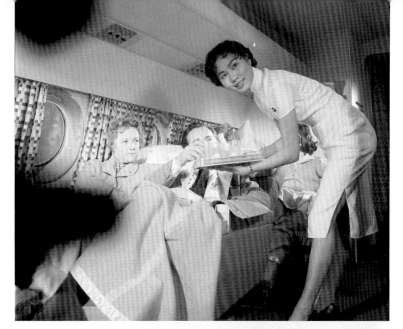

ABOVE **Jet travel in the 1950s was luxurious and glamorous. This picture was taken aboard a BOAC Comet 4 in February 1959.** *(DH11865C/ BAE Systems)*

RIGHT **Aerolineas Argentinas were proud of their Comet 4 fleet, and in spite of losing three of them in crashes, it was and is one of the world's safest airlines.** *(Aerolineas Argentinas)*

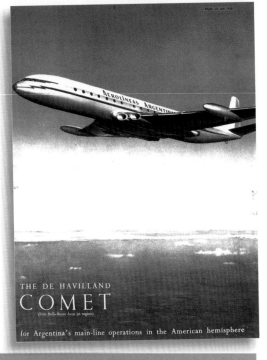

and Sydney. Within a year two of their Comets were found to have corrosion at the front spar bolts and were withdrawn from service; and in 1969 they sold all their Comets to Dan-Air.

Mexico: Mexicana – full name Compagnia Mexicana de Aviacion – bought their first Comet 4C in June 1960 as part of an order for three aircraft and launched jet services to the United States as well as within Mexico. With destinations that included New York, San Francisco, Los Angeles, Denver, Dallas, Chicago and Miami, the Comet proved so popular that the airline considered taking up their option on two more Comets, but in the end decided to lease from BOAC as and when needed, and the Comets they didn't purchase were instead bought by Sudan Airways. One of those was the last Comet built at Hatfield. Mexicana later sold their Comets to a New Mexico company called Westernair who planned to operate them as executive jets, but this fell through and three of the aircraft were scrapped. The remaining 4C (N888WA) went to Boeing for their Museum of Flight.

Portugal: Between 1959 and 1962, Transportes Aereos Portugueses chartered British European Airways Comet 4Bs to operate a service between London and Lisbon.

Saudi Arabia: The government of Saudi Arabia ordered a Comet 4C for the personal use of King Ibn Saud. Built at Hatfield, SA-R-7 first flew in March 1962 and sported a striking green, gold and white finish. It was fitted with a lavish VIP front cabin and the specification included special lavatories with gold fittings. It was destroyed in a crash a year later when it hit a ridge in the Alps south of Turin, killing all on board.

Sri Lanka: Air Ceylon operated a number of Comet 4s under a leasing agreement with BOAC in 1962 to operate a Comet 4 (G-APDP) for a weekly service to London and Singapore from Colombo Airport. They remained in BOAC colours, the only difference being that 'BOAC' on the fuselage was replaced with the words 'Air Ceylon', while 'BOAC' remained on the pinion fuel tanks.

LEFT **Long before airline liveries became wild and imaginative, Aerolineas Argentinas' Comet 4 (LV-AHU) displays her tasteful colour scheme.** *(Clinton H. Groves)*

ABOVE A moody shot of Aerolineas Argentinas' Comet 4 (LV-PLM) cruising between the cloud layers. *(Copyright unknown)*

LEFT With the Comet 4, Mexicana launched jet passenger services to the United States as well as within their own country. This is XA-NAS. *(Copyright unknown)*

ABOVE **Plenty of legroom in those days: passengers aboard a Misrair Comet 4C in 1960. The following year it became United Arab Airlines.**
(Copyright unknown)

maintained by BEA at Heathrow and were withdrawn from service in 1973 and sold to Dan-Air. Sudan Airways flew the last scheduled Comet service into Heathrow in 1972.

United Kingdom: British European Airways, having seen Air France introduce their short-haul Caravelle jet airliner in 1958, were determined not to be left behind, and de Havilland had won the order for an airliner to the airline's specifications – the Trident. But that aircraft – bigger than the Caravelle – would not be available until 1964, so an order was placed in the meantime for the Comet 4B, which turned out to be very successful. BEA flew their fleet of 15 Comets on their longer routes. Passengers loved it, and it returned a healthy profit for the airline until it was replaced by the Trident. The last BEA Comet flight was on 31 October 1971, but with the introduction of BEA Airtours it flew on until the end of October 1973.

BEA Airtours Ltd: A wholly owned subsidiary of BEA set up to exploit the rapidly growing inclusive tour holiday flights market, BEA Airtours was based at Gatwick and received seven of BEA's Comets when they were withdrawn from the parent company's routes. The company began commercial flights in March 1970, but by the end of the following year began to take deliveries of ex-BOAC Boeing 707s to replace their Comet fleet. In

BELOW **G-APMG was one of BEA's 15 Comet 4Bs that gave superb service; they were loved by passengers.**
(Copyright unknown)

Sudan: In the 1960s Sudan Airways purchased two new Comet 4Cs which were originally for Mexicana, and began operating early the following year, covering destinations from their base at Khartoum such as London, Frankfurt, Rome, Athens, Beirut, Cairo, Addis Ababa and Nairobi. Their Comets were

RIGHT Fuselage keels for BEA Comet 4Bs under construction in 1958. *(Copyright unknown)*

October 1973 they made their last scheduled Comet flight.

BOAC: The corporation purchased 19 Comet 4s and had the distinction of opening the world's first transatlantic service; and by the time the last Atlantic flight was made on 16 October 1960, BOAC Comets had made 2,304 crossings at an average of three per day and carried a total of 94,000 passengers. Not bad for an aircraft that, because of its size and limited range, was not particularly well suited for this route – especially when compared to the Boeing 707. Up until 1965 the aircraft continued to give sterling service on the more traditional schedules to South Africa, South America, the Far East, the Caribbean and Australia, although the corporation began to sell off their Comets in 1963 to make way for the bigger and faster 707. Their last Comet service was on 23 November 1965, and by the end of 1969 BOAC had sold all but one of their Comet fleet.

LEFT Perhaps not the best picture to promote Comet travel: the de Havilland photographer captures a group of glum faces on a BEA Comet 4B in October 1959. *(DH12313K/BAE Systems)*

BELOW Malaysia–Singapore Airlines Comet 4 pictured at Hatfield on 17 April 1968. *(Philip J. Birtles collection)*

ABOVE A lovely study of Olympic Airways Comet 4B (G-APYC) in April 1960. She later went to BEA, then Channel Airways, before going on to serve – as so many Comets did – with Dan-Air. *(Philip J. Birtles collection)*

ABOVE High above a massive cloud base, Comet 4C (9K-ACA) of Kuwait Airways. *(DH14217A/BAE Systems)*

Channel Airways: A private airline that made good use of the Comet was Channel Airways, which was based at Southend. It quickly graduated from giving joy rides in 1946 to charter flights two years later, and then on to greater things, culminating in the leasing of five ex-BEA and ex-Olympic Airways Comet 4Bs in 1970 and 1971. It had carved out a healthy domestic and cross-Channel market, basing its jet fleet at Stansted, but it was not to last: financial difficulties led to the firm's closure in 1972 and its Comets were sold to Dan-Air.

Dan-Air: Also known as Dan-Air London, the company bought all of the surviving flyable Comet 4s from the late 1960s into the 1970s. Some were for spares reclamation, but most were operated on the carrier's inclusive tour charters.

Considering they had started as an independent airline with just one Douglas C-47B Dakota in 1953, Dan Air Services Ltd had come a long way, and they went on to become the world's largest operator of the Comet for several years after they purchased BOAC's fleet – and eventually bought a total of 48 Comets of all types, some of which were used as spares. They continued to operate their fleet of Comet 4Cs until the end of November 1980, and between 1966 and the final flight they carried more than 8 million passengers. In spite of consuming twice as much fuel as the BAC 1-11 they had a better range and managed to weather the 1973 fuel crisis; and

RIGHT One of Dan-Air's huge fleet of Comets, this is a 4B (G-BBUV) pictured in May 1977. *(PRM Aviation)*

their impressive take-off and landing capabilities meant that Dan-Air were able to exploit their use from regional airports.

As well as operating a 24-hour charter service, Dan-Air opened up a winter service to the Canary Islands, which became very popular. Competing with the airline giants, they missed no opportunity to use the Comet to best advantage, making every use of its range and cheap purchase price.

The last Comets to be operated by Dan-Air were five ex-RAF 4Cs from 216 Squadron, which had low flying hours and entered passenger service in 1975. One of them, G-BDIW, made the last commercial Comet flight in the world on 9 November 1980, and several Dan-Air Comets survive at various locations throughout the UK.

Comet 4 military operators

Royal Air Force: Having had such success with the Comet 2 for transport and VIP duties, the RAF placed an order for five Comet 4Cs. With the greater range and seating capacity, these were seen as ideal to complement the worldwide operations already established by the Series 2. The order was placed in 1960, and the military version of the 4C was known as the C4, all five being built at de Havilland's Chester factory. A safety feature of the C4 was the

ABOVE Comet 4, XR395, was fitted out in VIP configuration by de Havilland and delivered to 216 Squadron at Lyneham on 1 June 1962. She is seen here towards the end of her RAF days at Akrotiri, Cyprus, in May 1974. On 29 August 1975, XR395 was sold to Dan-Air and re-registered as G-BDIT, before eventually falling to the scrap man's blowtorch at Blackbushe in 1984. *(PRM Aviation)*

rear-facing seats. After acceptance and crew training, the first aircraft, XR395, was delivered to 216 Squadron at Lyneham in Wiltshire in February 1962. By June, all five were in service.

At first the Comet C4s of 'Two-sixteen' were used almost exclusively for VIP flying, their guests including members of the Royal Family, a succession of prime ministers, government ministers and overseas heads of state. The special VIP fitting out for the Comet introduced a new style of long-range communication flights and a complete suite consisting of bedroom,

LEFT The last of the original 21 Comet 1s, XM823 had a long career starting with Air France. After modifications as a 1XB with a strengthened fuselage and circular windows, she took part in various research programmes. She is pictured on her last flight to Shawbury, Shropshire, on 8 April 1968 for outdoor storage. She is now on display at the RAF Museum, Cosford, as G-APAS. *(Philip J. Birtles collection)*

ABOVE **A fine study of a fine test pilot on his last operational flight. John Cunningham at the helm of Comet 4C *Canopus* (XS235) on 14 March 1997. This was the last Comet flying.** *(DERA)*

day room, office and staff quarters in the forward section of the fuselage. At least one of the squadron's five aircraft was usually in the configuration and ready for immediate use.

One of the most important roles for the C4 in the early 1970s was 'route activation'. The squadron had to have the capability of sending one or more aircraft at a moment's notice to any airfield in the world capable of taking a Comet.

If the RAF needed to send a force overseas, the Comet would fly out in advance, deploying crews and support personnel along the route if staging posts were required and at the destination airfield. This meant that crews had to be prepared to operate into and out of airfields not normally used by the RAF. The squadron also had to be ready to fly out as a back-up for passenger aircraft that had become unserviceable overseas.

The Comets remained in operation until 216 disbanded at the end of June 1975. The fleet then went to 60 MU (Maintenance Unit) at Leconfield in Yorkshire, with XR395 making a special commemorative flight from Lyneham to Leconfield via Heathrow and Hatfield. But the aircraft still had some life ahead of them, for they were to feed the voracious Comet appetite of Dan-Air.

RAE and A&AEE: With plenty of room to house test equipment and crews, the Comet 4 was the perfect flying laboratory, and three ex-BOAC aircraft were used for this purpose by the RAE. With its passenger duties over, G-APDF was sold to the Ministry of Technology with the serial XV814 and based at Farnborough with the radio department. It was later fitted with the larger Nimrod fin and rudder, in which guise it became known as the 'Comrod', and served until the end of 1992 when it was used at the Aircraft and Armament Experimental Establishment at Boscombe Down as spares for their long-serving Comet 4C, *Canopus* (XS235) which was the last Comet flying.

Farnborough acquired another Series 4 in March 1973, which was used for testing a wide range of equipment before being broken up after its RAE duties were over in 1973. This aircraft, originally G-APDP with BOAC, had already gone to Dan-Air before its new life as a flying lab with the serial XX944 – but It was short-lived, and it was grounded in 1975 with severe corrosion.

RIGHT **At one of her final displays, the last Comet (XS235) named *Canopus* shows herself off at the 1996 International Air Tattoo.** *(PRM Aviation)*

The final Comet 4 used as a test-bed was G-APDS, which was assigned to the Nimrod AEW3 (Airborne Early Warning) programme as XW626. It was originally purchased by the Ministry of Technology in 1969, and after modifications and conversions went to Woodford in 1972 for further work before taking part in extensive trials for the Nimrod. It was later fitted with a Nimrod nose radome and first flew in this configuration on 28 June 1977. As the Nimrods themselves joined the flight trials, XS626 was withdrawn in the summer of 1981 and scrapped in 1994.

Canopus, the last Comet: XS235, a Comet 4C, had a service life of nearly 40 years. Built at Chester, she first flew on 26 September 1963 to Hatfield to be fitted out with reference grade inertial navigational equipment in the cabin, and in December was delivered to Boscombe Down, where she served as a flying laboratory until retirement in 1997.

In all those years she clocked up a short flying time of 8,500hr, but as the last Comet flying she was continually monitored. However, it wasn't the airframe that led to her retirement: two of her Avon engines were nearing the end of their working life and there were no facilities to overhaul them. Her last operational mission was on 14 March 1997. On board was John Cunningham, who had taken her on her maiden flight all those years ago.

She was offered for sale, and a bid by de Havilland Heritage was accepted – but there was no room for her at the London Colney Museum, so she was flown to Bruntingthorpe in Leicestershire, where she is kept in ground-running condition by the British Aviation Heritage Group.

ABOVE *Canopus* **at Bruntingthorpe, her final resting place, where she is kept in running condition and carries out regular fast taxi runs.** *(PRM Aviation)*

BELOW The earliest complete Comet in the world: 1XB (G-APAS) at the RAF Museum, Cosford. *(Tony Hisgett)*

Chapter Eight

The Nimrod

From the Comet came the Nimrod.
Instead of being full of passengers
it was packed with sophisticated
avionics for its new military role. But
over the years, as systems became
more complex, more expensive,
generated more heat and needed
more space, the ageing airframe
began to show its limitations, and
although the Nimrod gave decades
of excellent service, the AEW3
became a massively expensive and
hopeless exercise, culminating in
cancellation. Then came a disastrous
Nimrod crash in Afghanistan, which
was the subject of a damning inquiry
that revealed the aircraft had always
been an accident waiting to happen.
The final debacle was the scrapping
of the MRA4.

OPPOSITE Nimrod R1 (XW665) of 51 Squadron on patrol far
out to sea. *(Crown copyright)*

ABOVE **A beautiful shot of XV226, the first production Nimrod MR1. She first flew on 28 June 1968 and put in 479 flying hours before entering service in January 1973. She joined the Cold War Jets Collection at Bruntingthorpe in April 2010.** *(Copyright unknown)*

The Nimrod, which was a military development of the Comet, was the first jet-powered maritime patrol aircraft in the world. But even before the Comet 4 was in airline service thoughts were turning in 1958 to an aircraft to replace the ageing Avro Shackletons of Coastal Command, which were themselves a development of the wartime Lancaster and had been adapted for maritime patrol and ASW (Anti-Submarine Warfare) duties – but they did not have the capabilities of dealing with the new Soviet nuclear submarines. They were also noisy and very uncomfortable.

CENTRE **Hardly recognisable as BOAC's G-APDF, this Comet was sold to the Ministry of Technology and based at Farnborough with the serial XV814. Here it sports a Nimrod fin and rudder. It became popularly known as the 'Comrod'.** *(Copyright unknown)*

LEFT **Comet 4 XW626 at an early stage of her tenure as a test-bed for the Nimrod's Marconi systems.** *(Copyright unknown)*

In the era of the Cold War there was more to the role than pure submarine hunting: the specifications called for air-to-surface strike capability against vessels, maritime surveillance, search and rescue missions, and enough space to carry troops if necessary. These demands would require a very versatile aircraft: one with plenty of internal space, long range, a high maximum speed and good handling at low speeds during the search segment of the operation.

After six years of studying various means of meeting the specification, a decision had to be made and the Comet won the day: it had plenty of internal space for equipment and it had a long range. But a crucial factor was that with its engines close to the fuselage it could fly and handle perfectly well if any of the power units

failed, and the advent of the powerful Roll-Royce Spey RB168 turbofan engine would give it sufficient performance to meet the requirements, as well as improved fuel consumption, particularly at low altitudes where many of the missions would be flown. The variant chosen for the Nimrod was the Mk 250 of 11,500lb thrust. Although larger than the Avons, no major redesign work would be needed to fit the Speys into the Comet engine bays.

By this time de Havilland had been purchased by Hawker Siddeley, and in 1963 it became known as the de Havilland Division of Hawker Siddeley. Design work on what would be called the Nimrod, named after the Biblical 'Mighty Hunter', began in the Manchester design office in 1964. An announcement was

BELOW The prototype Nimrod under construction. (Copyright unknown)

BOTTOM Used for Nimrod development trials over a period of five years, XV148 made its first flight on 23 May 1967 at Chester. It is pictured here at Hatfield in July 1970. (Philip J. Birtles collection)

ROLLS-ROYCE SPEY

Heavier, longer and of greater diameter than the Avon – but still less than the Ghost – the Spey was a turbofan engine that had military and civil applications. The principle of the turbofan is simple: a large ducted fan at the front uses energy from the jet engine to drive air rearwards, and some of that air bypasses the engine itself, so power is produced from a combination of conventional jet thrust and the fan. Turbofans on which the jet produces more thrust than the fan are known as low bypass, and examples include the Spey RB168 used on the Nimrod.

Rolls-Royce had already introduced a bypass engine as early as 1954. This was the Conway, which was too large for some of the smaller airliners, as was the Medway, so a down sized version was developed under a team led by Frederick Morley, which became the famous Spey. It had a fairly small fan which developed a bypass ratio of 0.64:1, and entered service in 1964 when it powered the BAC 1-11 and the HS Trident.

The RB168 version, as well as powering the Nimrod, was also used in the Blackburn Buccaneer carrier-borne strike aircraft.

ABOVE **Doing what it was designed to do: a Nimrod MR1 tracks a Soviet submarine in 1969.** *(Copyright unknown)*

flight crew's windscreens were enlarged and the nose was extended to accommodate radar equipment. Electronic Support Measures (ESM) equipment was housed in a fairing on top of the fin, while a 'sting' extension contained the Magnetic Anomaly Detector (MAD). This was able to detect extremely small local changes in intensity of the earth's magnetic field from the nominal value, such as would be given off by the presence of an iron mass of appreciable size, such as a submarine. When detected, the anomaly would show up as a blip on an otherwise flat trace.

A further aid in locating a submarine was a device called Autolycus, which was an ionisation 'sniffer' that could sense small concentrations of combustion products from fuel oils, and would thus indicate the presence of shipping – however, too much time spent patrolling a small area could result in spurious readings, as the equipment could also pick up traces from the aircraft itself.

Knowing that the Nimrod would stand or fall on the efficiency of its electronic detection equipment, Hawker Siddeley took over responsibility for the management and development of these systems, while Elliott-Automation's Advanced Military Systems division was selected as design coordinator for the nav-attack equipment.

made by Prime Minister Harold Wilson in Parliament on 2 February 1965 that an order would be placed for a maritime patrol version of the Comet, the HS801. The initial order was for 38 Nimrod MR1s (Maritime Reconnaissance), plus the last two Comet 4Cs (XV147 and XV148), which would be used for development and flight trials for the project.

No major changes were necessary to the airframe, apart from a dorsal extension to the fin, but to house the weapons systems the fuselage, which had been shortened to standard Comet 4 dimensions, was deepened, with the addition of an unpressurised ventral pannier that ran for almost the full length of the aircraft, and which gave the Nimrod its distinctive profile. Most of the passenger windows were removed, the

First flight

The first flight of XV148 as a Nimrod was made on 23 May 1967 with John Cunningham at the controls when he flew it

RIGHT **Nimrod R1s of 51 Squadron on patrol in August 2004.** *(Crown copyright)*

**RIGHT Nimrod MR1 (XV254) at Finningley in 1977.
To the left is another MR1 (XV249).**
(Philip J. Birtles collection)

from Chester to Woodford, and it was followed two months later by XV147, which was not quite a Nimrod in that it was powered by Avons to save time and money. This aircraft was used for developing the ASW system.

The first operational MR1 (XV230) was delivered to the Maritime Operational Training Unit based at St Mawgan, Cornwall, in October 1969. This later became the 236 Operational Conversion Unit, and was soon joined by seven more MR1s. The first squadron to receive the aircraft was 201 at Kinloss in Scotland, where squadrons 120 and 206 also began Nimrod operations, and the type also served with 42 Squadron at St Mawgan and 203 Squadron based in Malta.

The MR1 was never intended as more than a stopgap measure and much of the electronic equipment was similar to that of the Shackleton – but one major difference was the installation of advanced digital computers that would have the capacity to integrate with future system and sensor upgrades. These computers would do all the information-gathering, but decisions based on that information would be made by the crew, of whom the routine navigator was a key member. His job was to navigate the aircraft out to the search area and to plot radar fixes along the route.

Sitting alongside him would be the tactical navigator, whose task was to evaluate data from the information units. He could also be responsible for commanding an attack if the pilot elected not to do so. Information was processed by an Elliott 920B computer and presented on a 24in-diameter display. The computer fed steering information to the pilot's flight director and began a countdown to attack, but for safety reasons the release of weapons was not done automatically, but by the tactical navigator.

The flight deck was very similar to the Comet and was fitted with a Smiths SF6 flight system and SEP6 autopilot. Mach trim was standard and a yaw damper was fitted to give smoother flying during the kind of violent S-turns necessary in ASW operations.

ABOVE Nimrod MR2 (XV260) of 120 Squadron at Mildenhall. The squadron's distinctive insignia is well shown. *(Philip J. Birtles collection)*

BELOW Nimrod MR2 flight deck. *(Copyright unknown)*

ABOVE Nimrod MR2 (XZ285) of 42 Squadron basks in the Finningley sun. *(Philip J. Birtles collection)*

To the rear of the flight deck bulkhead were two hemispherical lookout blisters for visual observations, while next to these was the station for the two navigators. Further down the cabin were the radio and radar operators, while opposite them, and looking out to starboard, were the two sonar operators, known as 'sonics'. Bringing up the rear on the same side was the ECM and MAD station, and two further stations were reserved for future sensor equipment.

Weapons and equipment

The Nimrod could carry a formidable array of weaponry and life-saving equipment in its 20,000lb-capacity bomb bay. This ranged from torpedoes, missiles and up to 150 sonobuoys, to air-deployed dinghies and survival packs such as the Lindholme Gear. Used in search and rescue missions, the Lindholme Gear was designed during the Second World War and consisted of a nine-man inflatable dinghy with emergency rations and clothing in separate containers. It was still in use in the 21st century. For night-time rescue missions a powerful remote-controlled searchlight was installed under the starboard wing.

The bay could also carry mines, bombs, nuclear depth charges, the Sting Ray acoustic-homing lightweight torpedo and the AGM-84 Harpoon over-the-horizon anti-ship missile. In addition, the Nimrod could be fitted with detachable pylons under the wings to carry missiles such as the Martel, an anti-radiation weapon that was suited to attacks on shipping with its long range and heavy warhead. Other weaponry included the Nord AS-12 winged air-to-surface missile and the AGM-65 Maverick air-to-ground missile. Pylons were later added for the AIM-9 Sidewinder short-range air-to-air missile

RIGHT Nimrod MR2 (XV241) sets out on another patrol. *(Crown copyright)*

for self-defence – but these were used only in the Falklands War and not in normal RAF service.

Reconnaissance missions were carried out with a pair of downward-facing cameras, which were later replaced with high-resolution electro-optical types.

Operation methods

A Nimrod on a sub-hunting mission was but one component in an intelligence-sharing operation. It normally carried a crew of two pilots, one engineer, two beam lookouts (port and starboard), a route navigator, a tactical navigator, a radio operator, an ASV (air/surface-vessel) radar operator and two sonar operators.

Active or passive sonobuoys were the basic tools of a mission, and they were parachuted on to the water in a specific pattern. They detected underwater sounds and transmitted the bearing of the sound to a surface vessel or aircraft. The passive buoys provided a fix on the target in relation to their positions, while the active buoys determined the range of the fix in relation to itself. One technique was to use an active buoy as a datum for the attack by beginning a countdown as the aircraft flew over it.

Once a Soviet submarine was detected, the Nimrod's crew would pass the information to Royal Navy frigates and other NATO ships, which would then set up a continuous monitoring programme.

To optimise the capabilities of the Spey engines, all four engines would be running at the

start of a mission, but as fuel was burned off and the weight of the aircraft was reduced, the two outer engines would be shut down to conserve fuel. Re-lighting them for a quick getaway on completion of the mission was initiated by feeding compressor air from an inner engine to a starter turbine, which was more reliable than the usual ram-air method. The inner engines also powered the aircraft's two hydraulic systems.

Most of the submarine detection work was carried out over the North Atlantic, and with its 10hr endurance without refuelling, the Nimrod was ideal for the task, and any information acquired on patrol was shared with other Allied aircraft. But in addition to its Cold War duties, the fleet played a vital search and rescue role in civil and military incidents at sea, and throughout its long operational life at least one Nimrod was in a permanent state of readiness for search and rescue operations.

ABOVE Dwarfed by the Rock of Gibraltar, Nimrod MR1 (XV238) poses for the camera. This aircraft was later upgraded to an MR2. *(Philip J. Birtles collection)*

LEFT Nimrod MR2 (XV254) armed with AIM-9 Sidewinder missiles under the starboard wing. *(Copyright unknown)*

RIGHT Nimrod MR2 (XV244) at Brize Norton. *(Philip J. Birtles collection)*

BELOW In spite of the tail sting, fin-top pod and other excrescences, the Nimrod remained a thing of beauty, shown to great effect in this shot of XV241 in her early incarnation as an MR1. She was decommissioned at RAF Kinloss as an MR2 in 2010, and after being dismantled her front fuselage section was put on display at the National Museum of Flight in East Fortune. *(Copyright unknown)*

Nimrod MR2

The plan had always been that the MR1 would be upgraded with new equipment as and when it was developed, and this programme started in 1975 when 32 MR1s were converted to MR2s. The flight deck and general systems remained the same, but out went the Shackleton's obsolete ASV Mk 21 radar and in went the new Thorn-EMI Searchwater maritime surveillance radar. Other changes included a new mission data recorder and a new ESM system, which featured new pods on the wingtips.

During its many years of service, the MR2's electronic suite included:

- EMI Searchwater radar
- Ferranti 1600D computer
- TacNav – Tactical Navigation system
- Two UEL AQS971 acoustic processors and associated sonobuoys (each AQS971 could control 16 sonobuoys simultaneously)
- Anglo-Australian Barra long-range sonobuoy
- Smiths SEP6 autopilot
- MAD – Magnetic Anomaly Detector
- Yellowgate Electronic Support Measure pods
- AN/UYS-503 data processor
- Sandpiper Infra-red detection system
- Missile Alert Warning System (MAWS), coupled with wing-mounted chaff and flare dispensers
- Link 11 datalink.

In 2003 six MR2s were equipped with the L-3 Wescam MX-15 electro-optical turret. Project Broadsword, which was implemented in early 2006, introduced the capability to transmit real-time video imagery from the MX-15 to ground stations and commanders.

Provision for in-flight refuelling was introduced during the Falklands War (as the MR2P), as well as hardpoints for two Sidewinder missiles. In preparation for operations in the Gulf War theatre, several MR2s were fitted with new communications and ECM equipment to deal with anticipated threats, and these modified aircraft were given the designation MR2P(GM) (Gulf Mod).

The Nimrod MR2 carried out three main roles – Anti-Submarine Warfare (ASW), Anti-Surface Unit Warfare (ASUW) and Search and Rescue (SAR). Its extended range enabled the crew to monitor maritime areas far to the north of Iceland and up to 2,500 miles out into the western Atlantic. With Air-to-Air Refuelling (AAR), range and endurance were greatly extended. The crew consisted of two pilots and one flight engineer, two navigators (one tactical navigator and a routine navigator), one Air Electronics Officer (AEO), the sonobuoy sensor team of two Weapon System Operators (WSOp ACO) and four Weapon System Operators (WSOp EW) to manage passive and active electronic warfare systems.

Nimrod R1

With more space in the fuselage for equipment than the ageing Comet 2Rs and Canberras, the Nimrod was the obvious replacement for the RAF's electronic intelligence work (ELINT). Although the airframe was virtually the same as the MR1, the R1 did not have the MAD boom at the rear, and the avionics were completely different. Up to 23 specialist crew members could be accommodated to operate the 13 equipment consoles.

Three Nimrod R1s were built for 51 Squadron based initially at Wyton, Cambridgeshire, but later at Waddington, Lincolnshire. They were delivered in 1971 and 1972 for the installation of secret intelligence-gathering equipment before becoming operational on 10 May 1974 and replacing the last of the Comet 2Rs.

These Nimrods operated in secrecy and were rarely seen. Their task was to seek out the frequencies of hostile radar and communications systems so that countermeasures could be developed, and many of their sorties were close to the Iron Curtain during the years of the Cold War.

The third aircraft, XW666, ditched after take-off from Kinloss where it had undergone work at the Major Servicing Unit (MSU) in 1995. A starter motor disintegrated and caused a fire in the wing, and the pilot immediately put the aircraft down in the Moray Firth as there was fear that the fierce fire could burn through the main spar. The aircraft was scrapped, but all the crew were saved.

This incident happened when the three Nimrod R1s were undergoing a major modification package called Starwindow.

THE NIMROD AT WAR

The Gulf War: Three Nimrod MR2s were sent to Oman in August 1990 after the invasion of Kuwait, carrying out patrols over the Gulf of Oman and the Persian Gulf. In such a volatile arena they were fitted with towed decoys as added protection, and once the Gulf War broke out they were joined by two more MR2s. All five aircraft took part in night patrols, and were used to great effect in guiding air attacks on Iraqi shipping. Nimrod R1s also operated in the area from August 1990 to March 1991 from a base in Cyprus. Like the MR2s, they were also fitted with towed decoys and carried under-wing chaff and flare dispensers.

Afghanistan and Iraq: Nimrods were again sent to the Middle East as part of the British contribution to the US-led invasion of Afghanistan. Missions in this theatre involved the Nimrods performing lengthy overland flights for intelligence-gathering purposes. The outbreak of the Iraq War in March 2003 saw the RAF's Nimrods being used for operations over Iraq, using the aircraft's sensors to detect hostile forces, and to direct attacks by the coalition forces.

BELOW Nimrod MR2 (XV235) takes off for a mission in support of Operation Iraqi Freedom in March 2003. *(S/Sgt Matthew Hannen, USAF)*

The system consisted of two high-speed search receivers, a wide-band digital direction finding system and 22 pooled digital intercept receivers. New workstations were fitted for specialist operators in the rear of the aircraft. As well as Starwindow, the R1s were also fitted with a new 'Special Signals' intercept facility with a digital recording and playback suite, an enhanced pulse-signal processing capability and multi-channel digital data demodulator.

Nearly ten years later, in September 2005, the RAF announced that, following flight trials and testing, it had accepted a new airborne reconnaissance system known as Extract, which was designed specifically for the R1 and developed by the American company Raytheon. Extract operated by examining routine radio and radar emissions while providing electronic combat support to military commanders. It delivered enhanced automated capabilities enabling it to respond to current and future threats.

After the Nimrod MR2 fleet was withdrawn from service in 2010, the two R1s of 51 Squadron bade a final farewell at a ceremony held at RAF Waddington on 28 June 2011, a ceremony that concluded with a spectacular display by XV249. This aircraft is now at the Cosford RAF Museum.

AEW3

The Nimrod AEW3 project turned into an embarrassing and unmitigated disaster, characterised by insurmountable equipment problems, massive delays, spiralling costs and finally the whole programme being cancelled in favour of the Boeing 707-based E-3A Sentry.

The plan had been for the RAF to provide airborne radar cover for the United Kingdom by using existing MR1s that had low flying hours and upgrading them with a brand new GEC radar system and an equipment package developed by Marconi-Elliott Avionics.

Initial development work was carried out on a Comet 4, which was fitted with a forward scanner to prove the basic concept, and as trials looked promising an order was placed for three prototype Nimrods – but even before the project was under way the possibility was looming that the Sentry would be chosen instead. The British aircraft industry believed the Nimrod would do a better job than the Boeing for NATO's Atlantic flank, and it would also preserve European technology as well as 7,000 jobs.

However, press briefings in March 1977 gave little confidence when even the most basic questions about costs were evaded by both Whitehall and the industry. The upshot was that the industry said it couldn't reveal figures because the Ministry wouldn't allow it to, and the Ministry said it couldn't reveal figures because it would embarrass the industry. The only certainty was that the AEW3 project was going to be very expensive.

On 31 March 1977 the government placed an order for 11 Nimrod AEW3 aircraft, consisting of eight MR1s that had not been delivered to the RAF and three more that

RIGHT Not quite such a thing of beauty, XV286 is rolled out on 19 July 1980 for the start of the AEW3 trials. *(Copyright unknown)*

became available when 203 Squadron was disbanded after the RAF withdrew from Malta.

The first Nimrod AEW3 (XZ286) was rolled out in March 1980, and took to the air on 16 July, piloted by Charles Mousefield, chief test pilot at Woodford. With a massive bulge on the nose and an equally massive bulge on the tail, there was no mistaking it. This aircraft was used to investigate flight characteristics, while the next prototype was to test the MSA (Mission Systems Avionics) package centred around a GEC 4080M computer. This computer was designed to process data from the two radar scanners, the Loral ARI-18240/1 ESM system, the Cossor Jubilee Guardsman IFF (Identification Friend or Foe) equipment and two Ferranti FIN 1012 inertial navigation systems.

Problems

But problems soon arose. The GEC computer had what by today's standards was a laughable storage capacity of one megabyte, which could be boosted to a total of 2.4 via a data-bus – but it was nothing special even then. It couldn't cope, it was too slow and it soon became overloaded. Another problem was heat: when all the systems were working at full power a huge amount of heat was generated, and the solution was to dissipate it through the fuel system. But it was only half a solution, because for it to work effectively the fuel tanks had to be at least half full.

In spite of the ever-growing technical problems, the project continued and eight production aircraft were ordered, the first being delivered to 8 Squadron at Waddington in 1984 for crew training. But the AEW3 programme was way behind schedule: the aircraft should have been in service by the time the Falklands War broke out, so several MR2s were hastily modified to give airborne surveillance for the task force.

The RAF was getting impatient. By 1986 a figure of £300 million had been put as the cost of bringing the AEW Nimrod up to minimum standards – but the RAF wanted something rather better than 'minimum', and as one unnamed source put it, 'God knows how much money would be needed to bring it up to final

ABOVE Sporting huge bulges front and rear to house new avionics, this is XZ286 at an early stage in the trials. *(Copyright unknown)*

BELOW A close-up of XZ286's unsightly nose – and an even more ungainly one on XW626, which was trialling Marconi systems. *(Copyright unknown)*

ABOVE LEFT XZ286 shows off her fat tail dome. In the background is XW626 displaying to good effect her bulbous radome. *(Copyright unknown)*

ABOVE Nimrod XZ286 on early AEW3 flight trials. *(Copyright unknown)*

LEFT Tornado F2 prototype ZA254 and Nimrod XZ286 formate for a publicity shot. *(Copyright unknown)*

BELOW Nimrod AEW3 (XV263) in use as a ground instructional aircraft at Finningley. *(Philip J. Birtles collection)*

performance level.' At this stage the programme was five years behind schedule, with GEC bogged down in contract negotiations.

One major technical problem was the transmitter, which had to be redesigned owing to a power problem that led to shutdowns and run-ups, these causing noise greater than the ground clutter noise that the radar was supposed to handle. But even 18 months after the new transmitter was running there were still signal processing obstacles with which GEC were grappling.

As well as equipment issues and the difficulties of integrating so much complex avionics into the limited space available – the fuselage no longer had the capacity for the ever-growing inventory of equipment – the programme was beset with amended specifications and altered time schedules, and by 1986 the RAF were recommending to George Younger, Secretary of State for Defence, that six Boeing E-3A Airborne Warning and Control System (AWACS) aircraft should be purchased instead of the Nimrod.

The writing was on the wall, and in December 1986 Younger announced that the Boeing A-3A would be purchased and the Nimrod AEW3 programme cancelled.

Most of the Nimrod AEW3s stored at Waddington were ferried to Abingdon, with one going to Kinloss and another to Finningley in Yorkshire for engineering training. As it was not possible to convert the airframe back to MR2 specification, all the airframes were broken up as spares for the MR1 and R1 fleet, with the exception of the one at Finningley, which was later used for further development.

The Nimrod AEW3 scandal had cost the British taxpayer in the region of £1 billion – but the Nimrod would live on in a new guise that became involved in yet another fiasco.

Nimrod MRA4

The Nimrod MRA4 was more than an upgrade; it was essentially a completely new aircraft. But it became engulfed in a miasma of delays, spiralling costs, contract renegotiations and eventually a highly controversial cancellation.

In 1992 the RAF needed a new maritime

patrol aircraft to replace the ageing Nimrod MR2, and the proposal by British Aerospace – later BAE Systems – was to rebuild the MR2 with new and more powerful engines and uprated electronics. They would call it the Nimrod 2000, and the only parts remaining of the MR2 would be the pressure hull and empennage; everything else would be new. After possible contenders from overseas were studied, the contract went to British Aerospace: the aircraft would be designated Nimrod MRA4.

The project called for the new and more powerful Rolls-Royce BR710 turbofan engines. These required much larger air intakes, so a new and more efficient wing was built with the span increased by 12ft 2in and the area by 23%. Although the MR2 fuselage would remain, it was to be equipped with a new mission system that would gather and display up to 20 times more data than the MR2. This included the Racal Searchwater 2000R radar, which was said to be capable of sweeping an area the size of the UK every 10sec and could pick out a submarine's aerial or periscope up to 40 miles away.

The entire landing gear was to be replaced to take the aircraft's greater weight, new weapon bay doors would be fitted, as would a modified dorsal fin fillet, plus the rudder, auxiliary fins and the pod on top of the fin, which would house a towed decoy. The two pilots would have an entirely new instrument panel derived from that of the Airbus A340, with much of the information presented on seven full-colour

ABOVE Following the costly embarrassment of the Nimrod AEW3 debacle, the RAF opted for the Boeing E-3D Sentry. Six of them are flown by 8 Squadron from RAF Waddington, and an upgrade programme is in the pipeline to keep them operating until 2035. Pictured is ZH101, the first to be delivered in June 1990. With a normal crew complement of 18, the Sentry can scan more than 300 miles at an altitude of 30,000ft from its Northrop Grumman AN/APY-2 multi-mode look-down radar housed in the circular top-mounted radome. *(John Andrews/Pixstel.com)*

(Ronnie Macdonald)

glass screens. Flight aids included a flight
management system, collision warning and
surface proximity alerting.

Massive headache

Design was one thing; execution turned out to

be another. BAE found that the MR2 fuselages
were not built to a common standard: there
were differences between each one, and this
caused a massive headache when it came
to installing the new equipment, resulting in
spiralling costs and delays. Then, after the

RIGHT Nimrod
MRA4 (ZJ517) at the
2006 Farnborough
International Air Show.
(MilborneOne)

new wings had been installed on the first three aircraft, BAE found after structural testing that they needed strengthening in high load areas, particularly around the cut-outs for the engine inlets and exhausts. BAE said it would not need a redesign of the wing, but the work was complicated, and the in-service date was pushed back from 2003 to 2005.

As a result of these problems, BAE Systems were facing a £46 million damages charge, and MRA4 numbers had been reduced from 21 to 18, with the RAF saying the submarine threat had lessened. But there was no chance of meeting the revised in-service date, as the first of three development MRA4s (PA1) did not make its maiden flight until 26 August 2004.

The project lurched from one crisis to another as costs continued to soar and procurement numbers fell. In 2006 BAE Systems were contracted to build 12 MRA4s, nine of which were to be production aircraft, the other three for further development. But disputes over costs continued, and less than two years later the numbers were reduced to nine production aircraft only.

The first production MRA4 flew on 10 September 2009, and at that time the cost of each aircraft was put at a staggering £400 million. The MoD announced that the programme would be delayed until 2012 as part of defence spending cuts. By 2010 all nine aircraft were nearing completion, and in March the first MRA4 was delivered to the RAF for acceptance trials, the objective being that all the aircraft would operate from RAF Kinloss.

Still the problems were far from over: the trials aircraft had numerous technical troubles and was grounded on safety fears. But in the end it didn't matter, for on 19 October 2010 the government announced that the MRA4 programme would be scrapped, all nine aircraft broken up and the Kinloss base closed.

There was huge controversy, with the government being accused of 'gross vandalism' and of acting too quickly, while six ex-defence chiefs described the decision as 'perverse'. Many people, including those in high places, were horrified at the prospect of nearly £4 billion of taxpayers' money being cut up and consigned to the scrap heap. But the decision had been made. It was the final debacle in the long and troubled Nimrod story. Edward Lucas, energy editor of *The Economist*, described it as 'one of the most extraordinary fiascos in the history of British defence procurement'.

The task that would have been the Nimrod's

ABOVE Nimrod R1 (XV249) at the Air Salvage International hangar at Kemble, Gloucestershire, in November 2011. One of only four R1s, the airframe's main components were taken by low loaders to the RAF Museum at Cosford where they were reassembled by Air Salvage in 2012. Trickiest part of the journey to Cosford was the 38m long fuselage, which had to be escorted. *(Jonathan Falconer)*

**ABOVE Members
and guests of
51 Squadron watch
Nimrod R1 XV249
make its farewell flight
over RAF Waddington
on 28 June 2011 as
they stand in front of
XW664. The address
was given by Chief
of Air Staff, Air Chief
Marshal Sir Stephen
Dalton, who praised
the aircraft and all who
had served with
51 Squadron.**
(Philip Stevens)

has gone to the Boeing RC-135W Rivet Joint, a development of the old C-135. The RAF acquired three aircraft, the second of which was delivered in October 2015.

The loss of XV230

In a long career with the RAF five Nimrods were lost in crashes, the worst being the notorious in-flight fire on XV230 in Afghanistan in 2006 in which all 14 servicemen on board were killed. Two other accidents resulted in fatalities, the first being in November 1980 when an MR2 (XV256) crashed near Kinloss when three engines failed after a multiple bird strike. Both pilots were killed, but the remaining crew survived.

On 2 September 1995 Nimrod MR2 (XV239) crashed into Lake Ontario while displaying at the Canadian International Air Show. All seven on board were killed. After a slow flypast with undercarriage down, the aircraft started its final manoeuvre, the second dumb-bell turn. It turned to the right under full power before the flaps were retracted to 20° and the undercarriage raised. It then went into a climb and at 950ft, for reasons unknown, engine power was reduced almost to flight idle. Speed dropped to 122kt, well below the 150kt recommended and taught for that stage of the display. The aircraft rolled steeply to the left,

then began to level out with the nose about 5° below the horizon. Its speed increased slightly, but the combination of the low airspeed and G-forces led to a stall. Full starboard aileron and full engine power were applied in an attempt to recover the aircraft, but there wasn't enough height to recover and the aircraft hit the water. The captain had made an error of judgement by modifying the final manoeuvre.

Exactly 11 years later, on 2 September 2006, came the horrific crash of a Nimrod MR2 near Kandahar in Afghanistan. XV230 was the first Nimrod to enter the RAF on 2 October 1969, so had been in service for more than 35 years. On the fatal day it took off on a reconnaissance mission over Helmand Province with a crew of 14, and shortly after taking on more fuel in mid-air the pilot reported a fire in the bomb bay. He declared an emergency and very quickly took the aircraft down from 23,000ft to 3,000ft, intending to land at Kandahar Airfield. But the Nimrod was burning furiously, and a Harrier pilot saw a wing explode, followed moments later by the rest of the aircraft, which fell to the ground in pieces. Twelve RAF personnel from 120 Squadron RAF Kinloss were killed, along with a Royal Marine and a British Army soldier.

The dead were named as Gary Wayne Andrews, Stephen Beattie, Gerard Martin Bell, Adrian Davies, Oliver Simon Dicketts, Steven Johnson, Benjamin James Knight, John Joseph

Langton, Leigh Anthony Mitchelmore, Gareth Rodney Nicholas, Gary Paul Quilliam, Allan James Squires, Steven Swarbrick and Joseph David Windall.

A seven-month RAF Board of Inquiry into the accident was set up. Its conclusion was that the fire was caused during air-to-air refuelling by an overflow from the blow-off valve on No 1 tank, causing the fuel to track back along the fuselage and accumulate in the No 7 tank dry bay. Less likely was that the leak could have been caused by hot air damaging the fuel system's seals. Whatever the source of the leak, the fuel was ignited by an exposed part of the aircraft's cross-feed/supplementary conditioning pack (SCP) duct.

The findings of the inquiry were made public on 4 December 2007 – four weeks after another incident in Afghanistan when XV235's pilot transmitted a Mayday call after the crew saw fuel leaking into the bomb bay during air-to-air refuelling, similar to XV235. But this time there was no fire and the aircraft landed safely.

As fears began to surface about the safety of the Nimrod, an independent review was ordered under Charles Haddon-Cave QC. The report was subheaded 'A failure of leadership, culture and priorities', and its findings were a damning indictment that pinpointed serious design flaws that should never have been missed, and highlighted the sacrificing of safety to cut costs.

The review made it clear that the loss of XV230 was avoidable, and cited the Nimrod Safety Case, which was drawn up between 2001 and 2005 by BAE Systems and the MOD Nimrod Integrated Project Team, with QinetiQ acting as independent adviser. Haddon-Cave said it was the best opportunity to locate 'the serious design flaws in the Nimrod which had lain dormant for years.

'If the Nimrod Safety Case had been drawn up with proper skill, care and attention, the catastrophic fire risks to the Nimrod MR2 fleet presented by the Cross-Feed/SCP duct and the air-to-air refuelling modification would have been identified and dealt with, and the loss of XV230 in September 2006 would have been avoided.

'Unfortunately, the Nimrod Safety Case was a lamentable job from start to finish. It was riddled with errors. It missed the key dangers. Its production is a story of incompetence,

complacency and cynicism. The best opportunity to prevent the accident to XV230 was, tragically, lost.

'The Nimrod Safety Case process was fatally undermined by a general malaise: a widespread assumption by those involved that the Nimrod was "safe anyway" (because it had successfully flown for 30 years) and the task of drawing up the Safety Case became essentially a paperwork and "tick-box" exercise.'

The Nimrod suffered from fundamental design flaws, which played a crucial part in the loss of XV230. The review concluded that the original fitting of the cross-feed duct to MR1s and R1s, the addition of the SCP to MR2s and the fitting of permanent air-to-air refuelling modifications to MR2s and R1s were contrary to sound engineering practice at the time, and contrary to design regulations in force.

Citing the Nimrod disaster in a 2013 lecture he gave on organisational failings, Sir Charles (he was knighted in 2011) made this pithy comment: 'Assumptions are the mother of all cock-ups.'

THE CROSS-FEED SCP DUCT

The Cross-Feed duct was part of the original specification of every Nimrod MR1 and R1, and the Supplementary Conditioning Pack (SCP) duct was added to the upgraded Nimrod MR2s to supply extra cooling for the aircraft's upgraded electronic equipment. The purpose of the Cross-Feed/SCP duct was to allow high pressure, high temperature (around 400°C+) 'bleed-air' to be transferred between the engines and the SCP.

The review cited the Cross-Feed/SCP duct as posing 'a potentially catastrophic fire risk to the Nimrod fleet from the very beginning' because of the following design flaws:
■ Its location at the bottom of a bay closely packed with fuel pipes and couplings.
■ The design of the No. 7 tank dry bays, which were located under the rear of each wing root and which were prone to fuel pooling.
■ Inadequate insulation, which was vulnerable to fuel leaks.
■ The absence of fire protection in those bays.

The Cross-Feed/SCP duct posed two main fire risks. First, the duct was vulnerable to fuel and/or hydraulic oil coming into direct contact with its very hot metal surfaces as a result of leaks from couplings or other sources, leading to auto-ignition. Second, the duct itself posed a direct threat to the fuel system because an escape of hot air could degrade fuel seals close to the No 7 tank dry bays, leading to the escape of fuel and auto-ignition.

Appendix

Comet survivors

XK699/7971M	Nose of Comet 2 named *Sagittarius*. Formerly gate guardian at RAF Lyneham, Wiltshire, now at Old Sarum, Salisbury, as part of the Boscombe Down Aviation Collection.
G-AMXA/XK655	Nose of BOAC Comet 2, later Comet 2R. Formerly on display at Gatwick, now at Al Mahata Museum, Sharjah, United Arab Emirates.
G-AMXH/XK695	Nose of Comet 2R. de Havilland Aircraft Heritage Centre, London Colney.
G-ANAV/CF-CUM	Nose section. Science Museum, Wroughton, Wiltshire.
G-AOJT/F-BGNX	Comet 1A, complete fuselage, used for tests at Farnborough after withdrawal from service. de Havilland Aircraft Heritage Centre, London Colney.
G-APAS/XM823	Comet 1XB in BOAC finish, RAF Museum, Cosford. Earliest complete Comet in existence. Originally delivered to Air France registered F-BGNZ as a Comet 1A. Later converted to a Comet 1XB, she was used for many trials and airborne lab tests until her withdrawal in 1968 for storage pending preservation at RAF Museum, Cosford, some ten years later.
G-APDB	Comet 4B, originally in Dan-Air colours, now in BOAC livery. Imperial War Museum, Duxford.
G-APDΓ/XV814	Comet 4, BOAC 1957–67, then MoS. Chipping Campden, Gloucestershire.
G-APYD	Comet 4B, originally Dan-Air and made last civil passenger flight of the type. Science Museum, Wroughton, Wiltshire.
G-BDIW/XR398	Comet 4C, ex-RAF Nimrod XR398, then Dan-Air as G-BDIW. Flugausstellung L. + P. Junior, Abtei, Hermeskeil, Rhineland-Palatinate.
G-BDIX/XR399	Started as RAF Comet 4C in 1961, sold to Dan-Air as G-BDIX. National Museum of Flight, East Fortune.
G-BEEX	Comet 4C, nose section. Originally with Egyptair as SU-ALM, then purchased by Dan-Air for spares. North East Aircraft Museum, Sunderland
G-CPDA/XS235	Comet 4C, *Canopus*. Last Comet to fly. Maintained in ground-running condition at Bruntingthorpe, Leicestershire.
N777WA	Comet 4C, originally G-ARBB, then XA-NAT with Mexicana Airlines, finally N777WA with Redmond Air. Parque Zoológico Irapuato, Guanajuato, Mexico.
N888WA	Comet 4C, ex-Mexicana Airlines, now subject to comprehensive long-term restoration project that began in 2006. Museum of Flight, Seattle, Washington, USA.
5301	Nose of Comet 1XB, ex-RCAF. Canada Aviation and Space Museum, Ottawa, Canada.
Simulator	de Havilland Aircraft Heritage Centre, London Colney.

Bibliography

Davies, R.E.G. and Birtles, Philip J., *de Havilland Comet, The World's First Jet Airliner* (Paladwr Press, 1999).

de Havilland, Sir Geoffrey, *Sky Fever* (Airlife Publishing Ltd, 1979 and 1999).

Golley, John, *John 'Cat's-Eyes' Cunningham* (Airlife Publishing Ltd, 1999 and 2002).

Phipp, Mike, *The Brabazon Committee and British Airliners* 1945–1960 (Tempus Publishing, 2007).

Ramsden, J.M., *Sir Geoffrey de Havilland, A Life of Innovation* (Hyland DS Publishing, 2015).

Rivas, Brian, *A Very British Sound Barrier* (Red Kite, 2012).

Simons, Graham M., *Comet! The World's First Jet Airliner* (Pen & Sword, 2013).

Flight Global Archives 1949–58.

Reports

Court of Inquiry into the accidents to G-ALYP and G-ALYY (HMSO, 1955).

Haddon-Cave QC, Charles, *The Nimrod Review* (The Stationery Office).

BELOW Comet C2 (XK697), known as *Cygnus*, pictured in December 1956. She was originally ordered by BOAC as G-AMXJ, but the order was not taken up and she was assigned to RAF Transport Command where she operated with 216 Squadron. When her service days were over she was donated to the Wyton Air Scouts in 1973. *(DH10041M/BAE Systems)*

Index